The Blue Mountains have always had a great significance for me since my Mother told me about them when I was a child. For me the Blue Mountains meant Heaven and life was the journey to reach them and to go beyond.

My Grandfather was Governor of New South Wales and my Mother spent much of her childhood in Sydney in sight of the Blue Mountains ... she shared her memories with us, her children.

I remember a children's story book which I much enjoyed and which had the title of *Beyond the Blue Mountains.*

The story was of four children, two goodies and two not so good who were travelling through life to the other side of the Blue Mountains, their goal, their Shangri-la. They had many exciting experiences en route and each time they came to a cross roads with signposts I seem to remember that the naughty ones were apt to choose the most enticing sounding ways which promised the most fun, but the good ones tried to persuade them to choose the paths which led directly to the mountains.

A very moral tale and although I think we sided with the goodies in theory, I suspect we could more easily identify with the naughty ones. Fortunately there was a happy ending to the story when all four children arrived safely beyond those Blue Mountains.

Elizabeth Basset

Timidity: sculpture by Naomi Blake

Beyond the Blue Mountains

Wisdom and Compassion
on living and dying

an anthology collected by
ELIZABETH BASSET

Medio Media 1999

Published by
Medio Media
23 Kensington Square
London UK W8 5HN

ISBN 0 9666941 3 9

A catalogue record for this book is available from the
British Library

Front cover photograph: David Coulson/Robert Estall Agency
Illustrations: sculptures by Naomi Blake

Typeset in New Century 11/12pt
by Scriptmate Editions

Manufacture coordinated in UK by
Book-in-Hand Ltd, 20 Shepherds Hill, London N6 5AH

Every effort has been made to trace sources and provide
appropriate acknowledgement

All royalties from this book will go to the Charity 'Help the
Hospices'.

In a previous anthology, *Love Is My Meaning*, compiled by Elizabeth Basset, Her Majesty Queen Elizabeth the Queen Mother, said in her foreword:

> **"We live in a world of unusually rapid changes. It is no wonder, therefore, that thinking and sensitive people want to know what is fundamentally changeless — those who read this anthology will find expressed in these pages what in our hearts we believe but find so hard to say."**

These words apply more than ever to this new anthology by Elizabeth Basset.

By the same author:

Love Is My Meaning with a foreword by
   Queen Elizabeth the Queen Mother
   (DLT 1983)

Each In His Prison with a foreword by
   Hepzibah Menuhin (SPCK 1978)

The Bridge Is Love with a foreword by Sir
   John Betjeman (DLT 1981)

Interpreted By Love with a foreword by Lord
   Runcie of Cuddesdon (DLT 1994)

Dedicated to Rachel Heath

to whom I owe so much

This poem speaks to me of the four virtues which were so apparent in the life of Rachel Heath — simplicity, humility, honesty and integrity.

Rachel was leader of the Blue Pilgrims, an international society of men and women founded by Beatrice Hankey in 1902 and dedicated to making the world a better place to live in. The Society's aims have altered to meet changing needs and members now work individually and in community to promote peace and goodwill among those they meet.

'Love Triumphant' seems to me to be very much associated with those aims and it encapsulates Our Lord's life on earth in a remarkable way. Before I came across it I had always pictured the angel with his flaming sword guarding the gate of heaven against intruders rather than keeping it open for the return of Christ and 'Adam's return with Him'.

Love Triumphant

When Adam went from Paradise
In sorrow for his fate,
The Father set the sword of love
Across the open gate.

He placed the sword in the angel's hand
And bid him keep the guard,
And the cherubs paused in their ceaseless chant
To hear the Holy Word.

"By love alone shall the gate be held,
This is my perfect Will,
When Love brings Adam back again
He shall find it open still".

The Lamb slipped down from the heavenly throne
In haste the way to find

He stayed not even to ask for leave
For he knew the Father's Mind.

Swiftly he sped, nor did he wait
The flaming sword to dodge,
He darted straight through the open gate
And hid in Adam's lodge.

Long were the years of toil and pain
And fierce the fight with sin;
But wherever Adam made his home
The Lamb was hid therein.

When a star shone down from Paradise
To mark the time and place
The Lamb came forth from Adam's lodge
And men beheld his face.

Year after year the angel stood
Watching the earthward track,
And ever he held the open gate
Till he saw the Lamb come back.

His foot was bleeding, his eyes were dim,
His fleece was scarred and torn,
A cross was branded upon his back
And his head was crowned with thorn.

The angel dropped the flaming sword
And fell upon his knee
"Now welcome Lord to the gate" he cried,
"'Tis open Lord for Thee".

The Lamb passed into Paradise
Loud sang the Cherubim.
For he came not alone to his Father's throne
Adam returned with him.

Rachel Heath

Tuning the Instrument at the Door

Since I am coming to that holy room
Where with the choir of saints for evermore
I shall be made Thy music, as I come,
And what I must do then, think here before.

John Donne

'Hassan'

We are the pilgrims, Master, we shall go
Always a little further; it may be
Beyond that last blue mountain barred with snow.
Across that angry or that glimmering sea.

And as the caravan finally sets out, Hassan says.
Sweet to ride forth at evening from the wells
When shadows pass gigantic on the sand;
And softly through the silence beat the bells
Along the Golden Road to Samarkand

James Elroy Flecker

Contents

Acknowledgements

So many people have helped me in so many different ways in compiling this Anthology, but there are some that I will particularly remember for their advice, encouragement and expertise and without whom the result could never have been achieved. I have listed them in alphabetical order and they will all recognize their particular and invaluable contribution. They are:

David and Samantha Basset, Teresa de Bertodano, Giovanni Felicioni, Jonathan and Jutta Findlay, Martin and Davina Findlay, Laurence Freeman, Laura Hamilton, Muriel Maufroy, Teresa O'Neil, Lesley Walmsley, Clare Zeigler.

I am also most grateful to Naomi Blake and David Coulson for giving me permission to reproduce photographs of their work which has made so much difference to the book.

I would like to take this opportunity of thanking all those who have so generously given me permission to quote or reproduce their work without charge. This will benefit the charity Help the Hospices who will be receiving the royalties.

Please accept my thanks to all who have helped in producing this book.

Foreword

In the *Egyptian Book of the Dead* the human soul is described descending into the underworld for its final judgement. It is a simple operation. Our heart is weighed in the scales against a single feather; the feather of truth. The symbol is haunting and terribly true. Who has a heart that can match the unbearable lightness of truth? Who can endure such simplicity after the complications we make of our lives?

Elizabeth Basset has a wonderfully light and simple touch as she presents the truth about death from so many perspectives. Her own words, introducing the anthology which she has culled from years of reading, are themselves memorable and quotable. She is a friend, introducing us to many voices who have shown her the wisdom and consolation of authentic friendship over her lifetime. And, as she says, friendship is the great gift we need in the days of our grieving and also in the preparation for our own *rendez-vous* with the one absolute certainty our life holds.

The only unhealthy thing in considering death, as she reminds us, is that we in fact fail to consider it. If we allow the fear of death to trick us into repressing our consideration of it then death will attack us from the unconscious, as in our society's cult of horror and violence, which tries to expunge the fear of death by making it a sort of perverse entertainment. The repression of the fear of death will also splinter into hundreds of other fears and phobias which control us from the unconscious, hampering our freedom to live here and now in celebration of the gift of life: a gift composed of both birth and death. The wonder is not that we die — all of the greatest teachers of humanity have assured us that death is not the extinction we dread. The wonder is that anything *is* at all and then that it becomes more fully alive through death and rebirth.

I can remember a few of the most terror-stricken hours of my childhood as I read Bram Stoker's *Dracula* through the night, too frightened either to read or to stop reading, too frightened even to change the position in which I was lying. I was not aware of the great unconscious cultural fears this was expressing, but I felt the cold fear of death in my bones. Those dark hours before the dawn when the sick body is at its lowest ebb are often the hour of death; and it is often in these boundless hours of loneliness that those mourning the death of someone they love wake to face the irreversible anguish of absence. I like to think that many people will read or browse this book in those silent hours. I am sure if they do though, their fears will diminish, they will experience the light and truth about death piercing the surrounding darkness.

The truth about truth and one which we easily forget is that truth is not just a right answer to a question or the solution to a problem. It is the whole picture: question, mistakes and all possible answers, questioner and questioned. The truth about death is neither an easy consolation nor a cheap platitude. Elizabeth Basset shows the truth from many different perspectives even including something of the perspective we cannot see from this side of the "Blue Mountains". Not all these views are visible to us at the same time. We are creatures of the moment. How and what we see of the truth of death depends upon where we are presently at, where we are standing in relation to it: in the fear of our own mortality or in the pangs of bereavement. The many-sidedness of death and of our attitude towards it mean that many different voices, scripture, poetry, prose, prayer, even journalism, are needed to express it. One of the voices gathered into this truth-filled anthology will almost certainly speak to the reader at a given moment.

If one reads through this collection without any very heightened sense of death or grief it has nevertheless an important value as a preparation for death. We are prepared by innumerable little deaths every day as well as by the major transitions of our lives. In enabling us to see the deepest meaning of these preparations, and to see the kind of truth that only death can reveal, this book will be a true and trustworthy friend.

Laurence Freeman.

Introduction

I believe it is important for each one of us to consider death. I don't mean that we need to take a morbid interest in the subject, but rather that we try to look upon it as the final great adventure in life. It is the only thing in life which is absolutely certain and it seems to me to be a pity that it should be such a taboo subject.

Of course when one gets to the end of one's life death becomes more of an urgent question, but maybe we shall have to meet the problem earlier on in the death of someone we love very much and feel we cannot do without. I wish so much I had thought more about it when I was young ... I have since come to believe that it really is possible to help those who are dying. Cicely Saunders has said "We accompany them as far as we can. Then we have to let them go, knowing that they will be met".

Father Laurence Freeman, in a tape entitled "Death and Dying", says "At death's door only one person can go through at a time, but it makes a great difference to know that on this side of the door there is a loving presence to accompany you and to prepare you for the presence that welcomes you on the other side. That seems to me to be the real mission of the new caregivers in this field — to be that loving presence as fully and as humanly as possible". I wish so much that I had had these thoughts in mind when I have been with my dying friends.

In my research it has struck me most forcibly how many writers from all faiths have been appalled by the ways of the West in terms of allowing our people to die alone. The Jews, the Buddhists, the Hindus, the American Indians all seem to have more concern for their dying and their dead than we Christians. Somewhere I read that so often all we do for our dying friends is to go to their funerals.

In this collection of writings, I have included thoughts and letters from the bereaved. There are "cris du coeur" from the dying for more understanding and consideration to be extended to them, as *people*, both in their own homes and in hospital. And here are many suggestions of things to do and not to do from people who have become deeply involved with the sick and the dying. This is where the Hospices play such a vital and imaginative part.

With some hesitation I have quoted 'messages' from those beyond death which seem to me to carry the ring of truth. These appear to have positive and creative substance and manage to avoid the trivialities which so often accompany some of these intimations.

I try to think of my own death as the door to so many opportunities to share the best things we have experienced in this life with those who have gone before us into the world 'Beyond the Blue Mountains.'

I would like to conclude this introduction by quoting from a very courageous letter I have recently received, written by someone who is suffering and who has read the transcript of this anthology.

"The piece 'Death in the First Parson' in your book (page) struck this note with me, saying so well what I have experienced myself. When I was recovering from my third abdominal operation ..., I was surrounded by the 'tiptoeing extra specially unobtrusive' care of the kind nurses. I too felt isolated by their inability to share my shock and fear of dying. I was marvellously supported by one nurse in particular, an older woman. She sat on my bed and held my hand and stayed while I did all the usual brave talk bit, and stayed longer so that I ran out of bravery and waveringly began to express my fears for my sons, for my husband, and their lives without me, and she stayed on while the tears began to ooze out. Then she began to cry too and we put our arms round each other and I was able to admit how terrified I was for myself and for dying. She apologised for crying and said, "Well I'm not much of a nurse, I'm supposed to be cheering you up, and not crying!" But she was my very first opportunity to feel the support of another human being in my 'dying'. She was so caring of me that she could feel my fears, her fears, my pain, her pain. It was all one. We were as close as two humans could get when they stand at the edge of life's path as divergent as health and living or sickness and dying.

"There is so much I could say about your collection of writings. Every page held a new vista, a new way of looking at something or an encapsulation of a feeling, an experience of my own that I had hardly recognised … I would like just to say thank you, before I close this letter, for the 'opening of the door between life and death' that some of the writings have affected for me."

Timidity: sculpture by Naomi Blake

PART I

The Journey

PARENT AND CHILD

And the Mother of Jesus was there

Mary was there for Jesus from the stable at Bethlehem and before, to the foot of the Cross and beyond. She was there for Him.

I received a Christmas Card from Bishop John Hughes with the above words taken from a Mother's Union banner showing a simple picture of the Blessed Virgin Mary. The Bishop continued on the card:

"I found myself drawn to the extremely difficult but rewarding writings of Soren Kirkegaard. From him I learnt once and for ever since that the essence of discipleship is response. That is the basis of the whole story of the miracle of Cana. Being of an observant and sensitive inclination Mary became aware of a need and brought it to her Son. Anticipating what would happen she prepared the servants and said to them 'whatever he says to you do it'. Be there, take notice and respond."

"In the evening they will examine thee on love" said St. John of the Cross. "And I feel convinced that one of the questions that will then be included will be 'were you there at the right place and time with just the right equipment to respond to the call which God had already enclosed within the encounter and for which he had been preparing you?'."

Mary was there when they crucified her Son.

Were you there when they crucified my Lord
Were you there when they nailed him to the tree
Sometimes it makes me tremble, tremble, tremble.
Were you there when they crucified my Lord.

Negro Spiritual

23

Divine Paradox

Denis Duncan

Has there ever been such evil in the world as there is today? The answer must be "no" in terms of quantity (or is it that mass communication brings every human tragedy into our homes)? but "yes" in terms of degree. Human beings have always, and often with great cruelty, hurt and harmed one another. So far as children are concerned, nothing more monstrous was ever ordained than that royal decree whereby every infant boy under two years old should be slain. The massacre of children by King Herod, following the birth of Jesus is an enormity too awful to contemplate, yet it makes a crucial point for us all in our utter despair over human evil.

It was to a world which could perpetuate such an event that Jesus came, to preach, to heal and to love. Moreover when he who "went about doing good" was himself the victim of an outrageous act of wickedness on Calvary, he left his disciples in no doubt as to their duty. "Go ye into all the world" he said, "and preach the Good News to every creature".

Here is the divine paradox that gives us hope today. It is when the world can be so evil that there is need to proclaim the way of love. The deeper the divisions the greater the need for reconciliation. The more serious the illness, the greater the need for healing. When fear and hate pervade the atmosphere it is the more essential to encourage calm and to practise love.

If the NHS can recognise the need for spiritual sustenance, how much more should those of religious faith strive to build up spiritual resources. The ability to survive in the world in which we live and move today depends on personal conviction, inner resources and true serenity. All who believe are under obligation to do all they can to create such strength in others.

The Daily Telegraph August 10th 1996

The Hardest Death To Bear

The American spiritual teacher, Ram Dass was responding to a father whose son had drowned. The father was in despair: 'They say God is perfect but all I can think is that God made a mistake. I cannot believe that there would be any good reason for Him to allow this to happen'. Ram Dass replied in part: I feel such pain for the loss you and your wife have suffered. The grief that parents' experience over the loss of a child is perhaps the deepest grief of all because it seems to upset the natural order of things.

I suspect that though you considered his work on earth just at the beginning, for his soul the work was completed. Even the manner of his leaving was part of his work. For you personally, the pain is shattering and seemingly unbearable. You wake crying and find life now meaning less. Such suffering is what the personality would avoid at all costs if it were able. For your soul, however, it is an entirely different matter. For your soul, suffering is that which forces you to grow spiritually, and brings you closer to awakening to whom you in truth are. I realise even as I say all these things to you that it is really too much for me to ask of you that you understand the way in which the manner of your son's death was his soul's gift to your soul. I suspect all that seems topsy-turvy to you. But you did ask me how I understand such tragic events, and this is my truth that I am honoured to share with you.

Probably your suffering and attachment to him and sense of loss is felt by his soul. Although he now understands what has happened, why it had to happen the way it did and why you are suffering as you are. I am sure he is surrounding you with healing energy; and as you are able to quiet your mind, I suspect that you will feel it. It of course acts to your benefit even if you don't feel it. To the extent that you are able, sit quietly and just hang about with your son, talking to him as you normally would about the many experiences you shared together. In doing so, look to see the threads of spirit that pervaded each experience. Imagine that you and he are souls who met on earth this time as father and son. How many times in your years together did the love between you nearly rend the veil of mystery that would have allowed you to recognise the truth of soul that lay at the root of your relationship? It takes only a moment for two people to recognise their bond as souls. Souls know no time and now even though your son is no longer embodied, you and he can recognise each other.

The Natural Death Handbook: Ram Dass.

Laura, aged 18, was killed by a crocodile while swimming in a reputedly safe waterhole in Africa. Frances Campbell-Preston is Laura's grandmother.

A Time to Mourn and a Time to Dance
A Prayer for Laura

We are here to give thanks for Laura. To try to ease the pain for our loss by remembering all her ways.

How she was joyous, full of happiness and always alert to see and appreciate the funniness in life; and to resolve its discords with an endearing frankness.

How she grew up to love her independence and making her own choices. How she equally loved her homecoming, sharing her experiences, her adventures and her jokes.

How she had the exuberance and zest of youth, grasped life and all it offered her, especially in her love of art, music, acting and writing.

How she worked so loyally, caringly and imaginatively at school and at home through her sense of service to her causes.

How she loved fun, dancing, parties and friends.

How she was full of wonder, anticipation, trust and fear-lessness.

How she laughed so often and comforted us, and was our peacemaker.

Lord may we always remember her, be thankful for the gift of her and the
Beauty of her young life.

From the Service of Thanksgiving for the life of
Laura Campbell-Preston
at St Conan's Church, Lochawe, 10th May 1996.

This was read during the Mass in Thanksgiving for the life of Jane Margaret Fitzalan Howard

I thank Thee God

I thank Thee God, that I have lived
In this great world and know its many joys;
The song birds, the strong sweet scent of hay
And cooling breezes in the secret dusk,
The flaming sunsets at the close of day
Hills and the lonely heather-covered moors,
Music at night and moonlight on the sea.
The beat of waves upon the rocky shore
And wild white spray, flung high in ecstasy:
The faithful eyes of dogs, and treasured books,
The love of kin and fellowship of friends,
And all that makes life dear and beautiful.
I thank Thee too that there has come to me
A little sorrow and sometimes defeat,
A little heartache and the loneliness
That comes with parting and the word 'Goodbye',
Dawn breaking after weary hours of pain,
When I discovered that night's gloom must yield
And morning light break through to me again,
Because of these and other blessings poured
Unasked upon my wondering head,
Because I know that there is yet to come
An even richer and more glorious life,
And most of all, because Thine only Son
Once sacrificed life's loveliness for me —
I thank Thee God, that I have lived.

Elizabeth Craven

28

Here is underlined the isolation of the dying and the bereaved in a centralised society that has lost almost all sense of neighbourhood.

Isolation

Neighbours no longer share the loss

Because the elderly person who has died may well not have been widely known by the friends of those left behind, the grief of the bereaved is not shared. When someone dies in Ambridge, or in an African village, or in a police unit, an entire community feels the loss. But when most old people in Britain die today, only a few close relatives are still in touch to feel the loss.

Nor is this true only when the deceased is elderly. In a relatively isolated nuclear family in which outsiders have played little, if any role in child care, the death of a child may be a uniquely isolating experience ... Contrast this account by Miller after the destruction of the primary school in Aberfan; "one bereaved mother told me that when she lost her child the company she sought was not that of other bereaved mothers but of her neighbours. They might not have lost a child themselves, but she realised they had lost her child. It was the neighbours who had helped to bring him up, who had minded him when she went out, had watched him grow and had taken pride in his achievements. In a very real sense they shared her grief. usually though friends and neighbours may be sympathetic, but they do not know the child well enough truly to share the loss."

Friends in their thirties or younger may never have experienced any close bereavement.

So the bereaved today often are isolated, and may well report being treated as lepers.

Modern Death: taboo or not taboo?: Tony Walter.

29

Written by the widow of a high ranking German officer imprisoned by the Nazi regime in a Gestapo prison, after the death of her son. Her grandson became a brother in the Taizé community.

The Child

"When I was yet a child, my mother's hand held me along all the ways, the paths all through the wondrous land of childhood. And her hand was warm, good, firm, like a hand that would never let go.

Later there came my own child with his child's hand in his mother's hand. And my hand held his firmly, like a hand that would never let go.

Yet death came! It does not ask for what is really released. And its hand is cold and grips firmly.

If now your hands are empty because of death, do not clench your fist, or God cannot make good your loss. And if he does not do so now, in our time, he will surely do it in his eternity."

A Universal Heart. The Life and Vision of Brother Roger of Taizé:
Kathryn Spink.

A Child Ill

Oh, little body, do not die
   The soul looks out through wide blue eyes So question-
ingly into mine.
   That my tormented soul replies.

Oh, little body do not die,
   You hold the soul that talks to me
Although our conversation be
   As wordless as the windy sky.

So looked my Father at the last
   Right in my soul, before he died,
Though words we spoke went heedless past
     As London traffic-roar outside.

And now the same blue eyes I see
     Look through me from a little son,
So questioning, so searchingly
     That youthfulness and age are one.

My Father looked at me and died
     Before my soul made full reply,
Lord leave this other Light alight —
   Oh, little body, do not die.

A Few Late Chrysanthemums: John Betjeman.

"Charles" was a 'cot death' baby who died during the Second World War. The Irish poet Lord Dunsany wrote this poem in his memory.

A Child's Dream

For Charles
Born 16th September 1942
Died 6th November 1942

For seven weeks his gaze
Dwelt on a world as fair
As was in any days
Autumn entranced the air.

The beeches in the dim
Of evening were like gold
Earth was as calm to him
As in some tale of old.

Strange that his memory
Where all our troubles cease
(Wherever that may be)
Is of a world at peace.

Lord Dunsany

The Grief That Burns

Recently we spent some time with a couple whose eleven-year old daughter had been abducted and murdered. It was every parent's worst nightmare. There was no way they could control the universe. There was no way they could make it go away. Their pain was so extraordinary that they simply could not hold on to it, and their hearts were torn open.

Soon after the death they wrote to Ram Dass:

"We go on though we have no stomach for it. We try our best to be there for our two remaining children and that is also sometimes hard. We constantly search our own hearts and those of many friends and relations who have opened to us, for deeper understanding and new meaning.

"I see Rachel as a soul who was actively engaged in her work while on earth. Her last three years in particular showed me the flowering of a shining being — caring, loving, and reaching out to the members of her family and many friends and relatives, young and old. She was always giving little 'love' things to everyone. To make you smile, to help you to feel good, to show she cared. She had learned, somehow, to bear her defeats and frustrations and not to be intimidated or slowed by them. The petals were opening and reaching for the sun. She was not a clone of her parents. She was who she was. She was the best of us and the strongest of us. The wake of Rachel's death leaves the many beings who knew her and a surprising number who didn't, torn open to this 'teaching'."

When Ram Dass received this letter he responded: "Rachel finished her work on earth and left the stage in a manner that leaves those of us left behind with a cry of agony in our hearts as the fragile thread of our faith is dealt with so violently. Is anyone strong enough to stay conscious through such teaching as you are receiving? Probably very few, and even they would have only a whisper of equanimity and spacious faith amidst the screaming trumpets of their rage, grief, horror and desolation. I can't assuage your pain with any words, nor should I, for your pain is Rachel's legacy to you. Not that she or I would inflict such pain by choice, but there it is. And it must burn it's purifying way to completion … For something in you dies when you bear the unbearable. And it is only in that dark night of the soul that you are prepared to see as God sees, and to love as God loves.

"Now is the time to let your grief find expression — no false strength. Now is the time to sit quietly and speak to Rachel and thank her for being with you these few years and encourage her to go on with her work, knowing that you will grow in compassion and wisdom for this experience.

"In my heart I know that you and she will meet again and again and recognise the many ways in which you have known each other. And when you meet, you will, in a flash, know what it is not given to you to know. Why this had to be the way it was.

"Our rational minds can never 'understand' what has happened. But your hearts, if you can keep them open to God will find their own intuitive way.

"Rachel came through you to do her work on earth (which includes her manner of death). Her soul is free and the love that you can share with her is invulnerable to the words of changing time and space.

"As our friends opened to their grief, they opened to their love. They experienced Rachel at a level which they seldom touched before. Less and less, as they opened were they so caught in the forms which always separate parent from child, loved one from loved one. Instead the grief which spins and burns the mind begins to quietly and gently sink into the heart."

Who Dies? An Investigation of
Conscious Living and Conscious Dying: Stephen Levine.

The last words of a Mother to her son who had died from Snakebite.

Emanuele

I cleared my throat, swallowed my sorrow and spoke to
Emanuele my last words of love.

Only yesterday morning
We were laughing together;
Today I am here with your friends
To bury you Emanuele.

To bury a husband was hard,
To bury my only son is against nature
and a pain which words cannot tell.
You were but seventeen
yet you were a man already
and you could play with life
with a grown man's confidence.

You died knowing you were dying
but you were not afraid.

You were brave, and you were handsome,
you were intelligent and you were generous,
you gave love and you gave friendship,
and you had love, and friends.

You shared with all your smile
Your charm, your help, your enthusiasm
Your future was a promise
of challenge and adventure.

You were but seventeen
but wise beyond your age,
and now you know already
the answer to all questions.

I am asking: where are you really
as this is but your body?
are you now the hot sun of Africa?
are you the clouds and the rain?
are you this wind, Emanuele,
or are you the sky overhead?

I will look for you always
and I will see you in every flower,
in every bird, in every red sunset,
in every crawling snake:
as everything of beauty
will forever be you.

Anything young and proud
anything good and strong.

You were an extraordinary person,
your short life was extraordinary
and extraordinary was
your cruel, sudden death.

For us — who are left — remains
just to wonder
the reason for such a waste:

Where has all this love gone?
I hope your journey has been good
as you have already arrived.

Just one more thing Paolo wrote to you
one long-gone day:

"Fly for me, bird of the sun,
Fly high".

I love you.

I Dreamed of Africa: Kuki Gallmann.

The Depth of Sadness

Everyone in the village shared the death of Gordon's mother bearing her sixth child at forty-six. Here death could not be hidden or pushed aside. Here death was normal. The women were busy in their kitchens preparing food for the relatives and the guests who would come from the other villages. Two canoes, spliced together, bore the coffin carefully up the river. The older men went to the new burial ground, a mile from the village, to dig the grave, and the older boys followed them, cutting away the bracken, the devil's club, that had grown over the narrow path. Even the small children went into the woods to seek wild flowers and green fern fronds which the younger women needed for the wreaths. And Jim and Peter the carver, made the long trip to the residential school to bring Gordon.

On the morning of the funeral Mark tolled the bell, and the tribe gathered in the church for the service. When it was over, he left the church first, leading the way down the aisle, down the steps to the path, that led through the deep woods to the new burial ground. Behind him six men carried the burial box, another six following to take their places when they tired. Behind them single file came the tribe.

"Rest eternal grant unto her, O Lord, and let light perpetual shine upon her". Each man of the tribe helped fill the grave with a spade of earth while the women sang in Kwakwala and the children, tugging at their parents asked, "What does he say?" and though Mark did not ask him Jim translated.

"He says she was a mother of the tribe. She spoke little and only when asked, and the men listened to her counsel ... He says she was one of the first to choose her husband ... and he says that her husband as a boy, was the first to wear shoes, and that he hung them on a tree for all to see but did not wear them … And he says she was good."

I Heard the Owl Call My Name: Margaret Craven.

The True Light

Without thee I am bereft of hope
You are the star that guides my life
My thoughts, my deeds, are given scope
To do your will when fears are rife.

You are my strength, my God, my all,
Only through you can peace abound
Though sorrow has me in its thrall,
From its depth Your voice will sound.

Its spell on me has cast a calm
No earthly voice has power to give,
My troubled spirit feels its balm,
I am restored, once more to live.

Oh never through this world's dark night,
Forsake and leave me all alone,
I long and look for your true light,
Which leads me to my Father's throne.

Linda Collin Willeman

THE LIGHT OF EXPERIENCE

Auschwitz

At 14 years of age Hugo Gryn stacked bodies at the crematorium in Auschwitz. That experience was transformed into something astonishing, life-enhancing and noble. On the one level, his absolute commitment to inter-faith dialogue, anti-racism and ethnic understanding is completely understood and can be seen as a response to the experience. But there was something else to Hugo beyond his public stance. When you spoke to him, you were made to feel you were the centre of his life and that he really did care about you.

How the obscenity of Auschwitz which Hugo explained as Man abandons God, could prompt such a great love of humanity and such compassion is quite miraculous and astonishing. There are literally thousands of people not just devastated by the loss of a great man and a great presence - they actually feel that they have lost a close and loving relative.

Rabbi Hugo Gryn, 25 June 1930 — 18 August 1996

The Moral Maze

This year I celebrate 18 years of working in religious broadcasting. There are many outstanding memories, but for me, none exceeds a moment in *The Moral Maze* when a member of the British National Party denied that the Holocaust had taken place. All those Jews had died of cholera and related illnesses. Talk of gas chambers was propaganda. The response from one member of the panel was instant and devastating. "Look me in the eyes" said Hugo Gryn. Silence. "Look me in the eyes". More silence. "Look me in the eyes and tell me it never happened.. I was there. I saw it. Look me in the eyes."

Hugo's life was moulded by his experience in the Nazi death camps. I cannot begin to imagine what that experience could do to a teenage boy. When the Jewish community gathered together in his home in Czechoslovakia after the war, on the first Shabbat the Rabbi invited the youngest member present who had survived the Holocaust to read the Torah. It was Hugo Gryn. Lesser mortals would have succumbed to bitterness. The classic response is to lapse into silence, to refuse to talk about it. Psychologists have spent their lives coaxing memories out of survivors and their relatives. Hugo refused to go down that road. He embraced the experience. He was determined that never again would the world be able to close its ears and eyes while people were slaughtered because of their religious or racial origin. Auschwitz gave him a lifelong hatred of religious intolerance. He loathed religious bigotry and campaigned against it as only a truly religious man can. Faith for him was that religious space in our common journey where God and humanity touch. His journey was a Jewish journey. But his humanity enabled him to talk to people of all faiths and none.

Ernest Rea.

In 'Building a Better World', Rabbi Dr Julian Jacobs shares his reactions to a visit to Warsaw.

"Be Strong and Let Us Strengthen Each Other"

The most moving moments for me were spent at Treblinka, the site of one of the Nazi concentration camps during the Second World War.

So perfected were the techniques of extermination that at their height some twelve thousand Jews were murdered daily. From the moment the trains arrived the entire process of gassing, shooting the infirm and removal of bodies took no longer than one hour.

We were all traumatised. Everyone remained in complete silence, the horror being too great for words. After a while I led some of our group in reciting Psalms and the Memorial Prayer, and then many of us said Kaddish in unison ... In prayer I usually use the Ashkenasi pronunciation of Hebrew, but on this occasion I used the pronunciation of Polish Jewry down the centuries.

At Treblinka I felt more vulnerable than I have since my childhood, and my reactions after the prayers took me by surprise. It goes without saying that all the non-Jews with us were friends of Judaism and the Jewish people. It was from their presence that I gained strength and support. No two people think exactly alike and the way in which we put our thoughts into words differed widely. One young man told me it seemed to him at Treblinka that a hole had been bored in the sky. Another, a Catholic Priest, said that the most terrible thing for him has been the normality of nature. He felt that grass and the trees should not have been growing in a place of such darkness and terror.

I suggested a different interpretation. For me the normal

functioning of nature brought sanity into a place where there had been insanity. It gave meaning to the argument that attempts to prove God's existence from the design and order of the world around us.

... For me the beauty of nature, even in Treblinka pointed to God's presence there. We cannot know why God was inactive during the Holocaust but many of us are convinced that He was present and that He suffered with each of the victims in their agony ... I see the task of the people of good will to be the building of a better world where human dignity is respected and where every human life is treated as sacred. In the pluralist society in which we live our only weapons can be negotiation and co-operation. In this task we can gain inspiration from the words that Jews recite after concluding each of the five books of the Torah: "be strong and let us strengthen each other".

Rabbi Dr Julian Jacobs

Forsaken of God

The suffering and the glory of Messiah predicted

My God, my God, why hast thou forsaken me?
Why art Thou so far from helping me, from the words of
my groaning?
O my God, I cry by day, but Thou dost not answer;
and by night but find no rest.

Yet Thou art holy,
enthroned on the praises of Israel.
In Thee our fathers trusted;
they trusted, and thou didst deliver them.
To thee they cried and were saved;
in thee they trusted and were not disappointed.
scorned by men

But I am a worm, and no man;
scorned by men, and despised by the people.
All who see me mock me,
they make mouths at me, they wag their heads;
He committed his cause to the Lord; let him deliver him,
let him rescue him, for he delights in him!
They pierce his hands, they cast lots for his raiment.

Yea dogs are round about me;
a company of evildoers encircle me;
they have pierced my hands and feet —
I can count all my bones —
they stare and gloat over me;
they divide my garments among them
 and for my raiment they cast lots.

Psalm 22

"By Death Trampling on Death"

There is another aspect to death. I learnt it from a Russian lady, Julia de Beausobre, who as a young woman had been tortured in a concentration camp and had written a book about her experience called 'The Woman Who Could Not Die'. As she approached in old age her own physical death she said to me, "the moment of death will be the inrush of timelessness". We all have some knowledge of what she meant by timelessness. When we are relaxed on holiday and clocks and watches no longer tyrannise us, and above all when we are with the person or the people we love most and are no longer conscious of time, then another and deeper quality of life begins to take over. It is eternal, and the word "eternal" does not mean time going on and on for ever, but "timeless" — a quality of life not imprisoned in time. So Julia, as she approached the death of her body, was conscious of timelessness like a great reservoir of water held back by a dam, and she felt that now the frail little dam which was her body was breaking, and timelessness would come rushing in. Many people who are dying have a similar experience of some joy or somebody they love coming to meet them out of the darkness of death. My sister Marjorie said in the last moments before her death "this is going to be exciting" and her son, my godson, who died of cancer in his early twenties said "I feel that I am setting out on the adventure of happiness". As my first wife Scilla was dying, Cicely Saunders, the founder of the Hospice movement told me this — "We accompany them as far as we can. Then we have to let them go, knowing that they will be met".

The Dance of Love: Stephen Verney.

The following extracts are by Helen Prejean and need some explanation for those who have not read her book or seen the film.

Helen Prejean CSJ is a member of the Sisters of St. Joseph of Medaille. She was born in Baton Rouge and has lived and worked in Louisiana all her life. She has written an eye-witness account of the death penalty in the USA. In the postscript to her book we are told that since the first publication of the book in 1993 the States of Kansas(1994) and New York(1995) have reinstated the death penalty and Congress has enacted the Violent Crime Control and Law Enforcement Act(1994) which expands federal crimes punishment by death to about 60 offences.

Helen Prejean was given the name of Patrick Sonnier who, with his brother had been convicted of shooting a teenage boy and girl, strangers to them, after raping the girl. Patrick had been on Death Row for ten years and was now awaiting the result of an appeal for life sentence rather than death.

He was finally executed in the presence of Helen Prejean.

Helen Prejean felt deeply that capital punishment was wrong and the long wait on Death Row a travesty of justice. She writes:

'I cannot accept that the State now plans to kill Patrick Sonnier in cold blood. But the thought of the young victims haunts me. Why do I feel guilty when I think of them. Why do I feel as if I have murdered someone myself?

In prayer I sort it out.

I know that if I had been at the scene when the young people were abducted, I would have done all in my power to save them. I know I feel compassion for their suffering parents and family and would do anything to ease their pain if I knew how. I also know that nothing can ease some pain.

... Then it comes to me. The victims are dead and the killer is alive and I am befriending the killer.

Have I betrayed his victims? Do I have to take sides? I am acutely aware that my beliefs about the death penalty have never been tested by personal loss. Let Mama or my sister, Mary Ann, or my brother Louie, be brutally murdered and then see how much compassion I have. Magnanimity is gratuitous. No one has shot my loved ones in the back of the head. If someone I love should be killed, I know I would feel rage, loss, grief, helplessness, perhaps for the rest of my life. It would be arrogant to think I can predict how I would respond to such disaster. But Jesus Christ, whose way of life I try to follow, refused to meet such hate with hate, and violence with violence. I pray for the strength to be like him. cannot believe in a God who metes out hurt for hurt, pain for pain, torture for torture. Nor do I believe that God invests human representatives with such power to torture and kill. The paths of history are stained with the blood of those who have fallen victim to "God's Avengers". Kings, Popes and military generals and heads of State have killed claiming God's blessing, God's authority. I do not believe in such a God.

In sorting out my feelings and beliefs, there is however one piece of moral ground of which I am absolutely certain: if I were to be murdered I would not want my murderer executed. I would not want my death avenged Especially by Government which can't be trusted to control its own bureaucrats or collect taxes equitably or fill a pothole, much less decide which of its citizens to kill.

Dead Man Walking: Helen Prejean.

Waiting for word from the Pardon Board as to whether a stay of execution has been granted for Pat Sonnier.

"No word yet" I tell him. Would you like to pray? He nods his head. I don't remember the exact words of the prayer — a prayer I am sure of essentials, forgiveness, courage, sustenance for this final big step if it should come.

When the prayer is over I say to him, "If you die I want to be with you". He says "No, I don't want you to see it".

I say "I can't bear the thought that you would die without one loving face. I will be the face of Christ for you. Just look at me". He says "it's terrible to see. I don't want to put you through that. It could break you. It could scar you for life".

I know that it will terrify me. How could it not terrify me? But I feel strength and determination. I will tell him that it won't break me, that I have plenty of love and support in my life. "God will give me the grace", I tell him.

He consents. He shakes his head. It is decided that I will be there with him if he dies.

Dead Man Walking: Helen Prejean.

Final Communion for the condemned prisoner on Death Row.

The Body of Christ

The old Priest says prayers in Latin and takes the communion wafer from the container and places it on Pat's tongue, then into my outstretched hands.

"The Body of Christ", he says. "Amen".

Yes, in this place I believe you are here, Oh Christ, you who sweat blood and who prayed aloud and in silent tears for your Father to remove your own suffering. This man about to die is not innocent, but he is human, and that is enough to draw you here.

Dead Man Walking: Helen Prejean.

A testimony by Jane Ewart-Biggs whose husband Christopher was shot in 1976 by the IRA while serving as British Ambassador to Dublin.

During my short life in Ireland I learned a little of the beauty of the place. I also came into contact with the sorrow of the North. Then its sorrow became my sorrow. I lost what was closest to me, as so many there have done ... At the beginning of July we set off for Dublin and went with great joy, hope and determination. Joy to be going to a beautiful country with a talented and articulate people. Hope that we could contribute towards a solution to its problems, and determination that we could succeed. There had been a lot of publicity about Christopher beforehand. He had a very clear idea of what he wanted to achieve there. I fully shared these beliefs — as indeed I did all his ideas. Four days after we arrived he presented his credentials.

... In the little press conference he gave, the day before he was killed, to get to know the members of the Dublin Press Corps, he outlined the way he saw his mission there and ended by saying: "I see my role here as an exercise in clarification. I do not believe in the diplomacy of evasion. I very much do not believe in diplomats being cut off from the life of the country in which they live. My political philosophy belongs somewhere on the centre left ... things I saw in Algeria and in the War have given me one strong prejudice — a prejudice against violence".

The day after, an act of violence — coming from a background of hatred and bitterness — destroyed him. He was on the way to the Embassy and a land-mine placed under the road, blew up his car, killing him and Judith Cook from the Northern Ireland Office, and seriously injuring the other occupant of the car; the driver. My first thoughts — I have lost my husband, the person I admired most in the world; I have lost the kindness, tolerance, humour and intelligence which he symbolised for me. Gone also is the work he intended to do for

Ireland. Then I thought how dreadful if his assassination could impair relations between the British and Irish Governments. The relations which he had so hoped to work towards strengthening. And then I thought I could salvage something … I could voice his hopes for Ireland and continue to work towards making his beliefs and ideals grow stronger.

There was a very moving memorial service for him set in the grandeur of St Patrick's Cathedral.

… The day of the Memorial Service I made a short statement on Irish television. "So many of you have shown sympathy not only towards myself but to the children as well. And I think many of you will have read that Christopher was a person who was particularly shocked by violence. And from the hundreds, and hundreds of letters of sympathy that I have from people in Ireland, I think you too are appalled by violence. None of us can afford to be equivocal about violence. Christopher was destroyed by it. But I am sure that his death will not be in vain, and I hope it will make us more determined to work for these ideals which we share with him. I feel no bitterness but I ask you to remember these convictions which he had and felt so passionately and which, more than anything else, I want to see bearing fruit.

The response from the Irish people was overwhelming. I got even more letters. They wrote in their thousands — they wrote to tell me their grief, their sorrow, their shame. And they expressed this with an eloquence, a passion that only the Irish can show. One person wrote — almost illegibly — "You may be weeping your lost husband but we are weeping our lost honour".

The Light of Experience BBC 13 December 1976

Understanding

With the pain
which I did not know before
comes the understanding
of so many things
your courage,

your many moments of distress,
when all at once
your resourceful
wit and wistfulness
would cut the string
and we could laugh again,
How,
tell me how
shall I cope
with your everlasting absence?

Requiem: Margrit Dahn.

The following poem lays a great responsibility upon those of us who have benefited so immeasurably from the peace and freedom which so many of us enjoy and which the young soldiers won for us by their deaths. It is surely up to us to complete what they began and thus fulfil their hopes.

Peace

The young soldiers do not speak.
Nevertheless they are heard in the still house,
who has not heard them?

They have a silence that speaks for them at night
and when the clock counts.

They say; we have given our lives, but until it is
finished no one can know what our lives gave.

They say; our deaths are not ours, they are yours;
they will mean what you make them.

They say; Whether our lives and our deaths are for
peace and a new hope or for nothing we cannot say;
it is you who must say this.

They say; we leave you our deaths. Give them their
meaning. We were young they say. We have died,
remember us.

The Gates of Heaven.

The World's Peace

May the memory of two world wars strengthen
our efforts for peace.
May the memory of those who died inspire our
service to the living.
May the memory of a past destruction move us to
build for the future.
May the first two atomic bombs be
the last two also.
May the first two world wars be also
the last world wars.
O God of peace
O Father of souls
O Builder of the Kingdom of Love.

                                    George Appleton.

This quotation I found in an exhibition of Japanese photography at the Barbican gallery. It introduced a series of photographs of the results of the nuclear bomb dropped on Hiroshima. All they could show was the imprint of the bodies of 'people' embedded in the rock for all time, their memorial.

It almost seemed wrong for me to be looking at them. All one could do was to try to remember that countless lives had been saved by this horror and to pray that because of the threat of nuclear warfare, this should never, never, happen again.

Hiroshima — The End of History

"There was not a cloud in the sky over the Japanese archipelago on the day Japan surrendered. There was a marvellous silence, the passage of time halted, more, it was the end of history.

"All sounds around us and all dangers, all that so clearly constituted the future we had been taught(and were certain) was just beyond the horizon, it all disappeared, disappeared into that void in the midst of which I stood, in my tracks. And I looked up on that beautiful summer day and all I could see was a vast, tranquil, deep blue sky.

"As my gaze returned to earth, my widened eyes beheld as far as I could see, an almost uniform plane, broken, jagged, charred and burnt, all ruins."

Architectural Apocalypse: Ryjimoto

Of course I have known about this for years, we all have, but somehow the visual record was for me so much more horrifying and real than the written word.

The Caucasus

A memorial representing a flight of seven Cranes, commemorating seven Ossetian brothers born in the nearby village and all killed in the last war.

The brothers whose memory is still proudly cherished locally, are the subject of some famous lines by the poet Rasul Gamzatov from neighbouring Daghestan.

"I sometimes think that warriors brave
Who met their death in bloody fight
Were never buried in a grave
But roam as Cranes with plumage white.

Since then until this very day.
They pass high overhead and cry.
Is that not why we often gaze
In silence as the Cranes go by?"

Portrait of the Soviet Union: Fitzroy Maclean.

The Shadow Self

My experience in Germany and during the War brought death very close to me, but I think it wasn't something I was particularly conscious of. That changed radically in my work with AIDS and the way that I think about death now is as a kind of paradox, as the light and shadow part of self. I often find myself centring on a line from Ignatian prayer which says: "On each of my dyings shed your light and love". I see death and resurrection very much as a process in my own life, and in my own experience in my own daily dying, the pain of that process is something that I'm very conscious of. The death of relationships. The new growth of relationships. The death of my ambitions and the letting go of things that are no longer important. So much freedom and new life has grown out of that.

Eva Heymann — German Roman Catholic Nun.

My Brother

Brother's death really brought death home to me. He and I were very close and it was an extremely difficult time when he was dying.

... His death brought me very close to what death is all about. It made me realise the horror of death too and my own fear of it. Dick was a very spiritual man but he didn't belong to any particular church and he had had an extremely difficult and painful life in many ways, so there was a lot of unfinished business in his life. But I was also aware of his letting go ...

That death touched me very deeply. Losing him was the closest personal loss I've had, and my anger with God, my anger with all the unfinished business and sadness in his life — that was with me for a good year or two. And each time I see the horror of physical mutilation, physical diminishment, on the AIDS scene it's deep anguish. Though I can echo what a father said when he saw his son dying. The boy's mother and lover were supporting him with their hands behind his pillow and trying to lift him to ease his breathing, and the father was at the foot of the bed. And the father said to me the next morning: "You know you may think this is silly, but when I looked at George I looked at Christ". And to me the whole thing was just a Calvary scene. It is repeated many, many times, and it's always awesome and a privilege to be there ... In all the grief work of the following year, 'being there' becomes the kind of focal point. I think that 'being there' has become a crucial meaningful, living phrase for me. Because being there at death also means that we can share the faith in resurrection, which may not come for a year or two — often longer — but there usually comes a point sooner or later when it happens for somebody bereaved, somebody grieving.

Eva Heymann — German Roman Catholic Nun.

The Love They Yearned For

I want to speak about my friends with AIDS. I think of them every day. Some I know personally, some I know because they are friends of friends of mine, and many I know because of what is written by them or about them.. From the outset of this horrendous epidemic, I have felt very close to the many young men and women who live with Aids. They all know that they cannot live long and that they will die difficult and often painful deaths. I want so much to help them, be with them, console them and comfort them. I am overwhelmed by the tragedy that, in their desperate desire to be embraced and cared for, many have found illness and death instead. I cry out to heaven saying: Why, O God, does the human search for communion and intimacy lead to separation and anguish? Why are so many young people who simply want to be loved, languishing in hospitals and lonely rooms? Why are love and death so close to each other'? Maybe the 'why'? is not what is important. Important are the men and women with their beautiful names and beautiful faces who wonder why they didn't find the love they yearned for. I feel very close to them because their pain is not far from mine. I too want to love and be loved. I too have to die. I too know that mysterious connection between my heart's yearning for love and my heart's anguish. In my heart I want to embrace and hold all these people who are dying hungry for love.

Our Greatest Gift. A Meditation on Dying and Caring:
Henri J.M. Nouwen.

If I Had Only One Sermon to Preach

Today I was called on the bleep to one of the H.I.V Wards. As usual I spoke to the nurse first, in order to find out the facts of the situation and the prognosis of the patient involved. She told me of Chris, a twenty four year old man (he was my age) who had just been admitted. He had been H.I.V antibody positive for about two years and had been in the ward for periodic treatment during this time. He had no partner but had been looked after by his parents — aged I guess, in their mid-fifties.

Chris was now very ill, with Kaposi's Sarcoma Lymphoma and Dementia. I was told that the doctors had decided not to treat Chris. He was so acutely ill that there was little they could do except prolong the diseased life. The decision had only just been made and the parents were going to be told shortly. The parents had made it clear up till now, though, that treatment should always continue up to the very last minute. It was not going to be an easy task to help them accept the reality of the situation. The nurse had called for a chaplain to be around knowing that the family was at least nominally Anglican.

When I entered Chris's room I saw how ill he was. The K.S lesions disfigured his appearance and his dementia was obvious. Sitting on either side of the bed were his parents. We talked a little and I spoke to Chris holding his hand and telling him who I was. I think he probably registered something of that. His parents went out to see the doctors and I was left alone with Chris. We sat silently together holding hands and sometimes hugging. We had only just met but we both knew that Chris had little time left to live. I tried to pray silently but was unable. I too was angry. Why had God allowed this suffering? Chris was only a year older than me and at most had a couple of days to live.

When the parents returned I held them and listened as they cried and spoke of their frustration and their disappearing hopes for their son. "I used to believe in God" Chris's mother raged at me. "I find it so difficult now". All I could say quietly to her was "So do I". Instantly she looked at me and her anger towards me seemed to go. "I'm so pleased … so pleased you've said that" she replied.

Fr Mark Oakley

I Heard The Owl Call My Name

A young priest is sent by his Bishop to Kingcome Village, British Columbia to minister to the Indians. The priest is not aware that he has only three years to live, but the Bishop is, and sends him where he will be able to live deeply the short time remaining to him. The reader becomes closely acquainted with these Indians: their daily activities, their myths, their character, what they were and what they are becoming. The book speaks of life and death, of union and disunion. The young priest dies, but not before he has touched the Indians with his care, and not before he has learnt something of their wisdom. A story which cannot fail to touch and inspire the reader.

The doctor said to the Bishop. "So you see, my lord, your young ordinand can live no more than three years and doesn't know it. Will you tell him, and what will you do with him?

The Bishop said to the Doctor, "Yes I'll tell him but not yet. If I tell him now he'll try too hard. How much time has he for an active life". "A little less than two years if he's lucky." "So short a time to learn so much? It leaves me no choice. I shall send him to my hardest parish. I shall send him to Kingcome on patrol of the Indian villages." "Then I hope you'll pray for him, my lord."

But the Bishop only answered gently that it was where he would wish to go if he were young again, and in the ordinand's place.

All day long he moved down the longest, the loveliest of all the inlets, and it seemed to him that something strange had happened to time. When he had first come to the village, it was the future that loomed huge, so much to plan. So much to learn. Then it was the present that had consumed him — each day with all its chores and never enough hours to do them. Now time had lost all contours. He seemed to see it as the raven or the bald eagle, flying high over the village, must see the part of the river that had passed the village, that had not yet reached the village, one and the same.

All day long on his way back to Kingcome, because he was alone and receptive, the little questions, the observations he had pushed deep within him began to rise slowly toward the door of the conscious mind which was almost ready to open to receive them, and give them words: You are tired. You have told yourself that it was due to the winter which was hard on everyone. Deep inside haven't you known that it was more than this? When the Bishop came to the potlatch and lingered after the others had gone and went into the church by himself, didn't you guess then it had something to do with you. And your sister? When you took the boys down and lunched with her, did you not see the sadness in her eyes? And in the hospital don't you remember the doctor's face, the look of quiet resignation upon it and the way he hesitated an instant before answering your questions? And when the Bishop first told you of the village, how carefully he did so. Did you not think "He is anxious I should go there. Why?"

It was dusk when he entered Kingcome Inlet and moored the boat at the float, and climbed into the speed boat. When he entered the river the stars were shining, the moon bright also and he went slowly.

Soon the huge flights of snow geese would fly over the river on their way back to the nesting place, the spring swimmer would come up the river to the Clearwater, and on the river pairs of cocky, small red-necked saw-bills would rest. The Father flying off when Mark passed and the mother pretending she had a broken wing to lead him away from her little ones. And each would feel the pull of the earth and know his small place upon it as did the Indian in his village.

He went slowly up the river. In front of the vicarage he anchored the boat and waded ashore. He trudged up the black sands to the path and stopped. From the dark spruce he heard an owl call — once, and again — and the questions that had been rising all day long reached the door of his mind and opened it. He went up the path and the steps through the living room and into the kitchen. The lights were on. At the stove Marta was preparing his dinner. "Marta, something strange happened tonight. On the bank of the river I heard the owl call my name," and it was a question asked, an answer he sought.

She did not say "Nonsense, it was my name the owl called, and I am old and with me it does not matter, "She did not say, "Its true you're thin and white, but who is not? It has no importance."

She turned, spoon still in her hand, lifting her sweet kind face with its network of tiny wrinkles, and she answered his question as she would have answered any other.

She said, "Yes, my son."

I Heard The Owl Call My Name: Margaret Craven.

Bernard

R. has just told me that Bernard (a priest and a friend, a wonderful, remarkable, generous man of action who gave his all) has died, defeated by depression. He committed suicide. Stupefied and shattered, I could only think: 'Bernard, why? tonight I ask myself: Why did they let him do it? We are all responsible.

Bernard died exhausted, used up, pushed to his limits, unable to regain control of himself, like a boxer at the end of a fight who can't find his corner in the ring and has to be helped back.

But no one had known, no one had seen, no one had come. Why? Why?

Wounded by the suffering of others and by life's ironies, his vision had clouded a little; crushed by the weight of his own generosity, annihilated by tranquillisers, over-excited by uppers, he couldn't last much longer. What other pressures and harassments did he suffer that we don't know about? I don't know. It no longer matters. What matters now, and what I am sure of, is that Bernard died because he lacked a little, or large, touch of friendship which dispels loneliness and makes a heavy burden seem much lighter for being shared.

… I'm going to the funeral.

Father D's very touching homily restores the essential to my heart, beyond my blind and futile revolt. It's true that a shining light springs out of St. Paul's text: baptised in Jesus Christ … in his death were we baptised … we are in communion with him through a death similar to his; we will be in communion again through a resurrection similar to his … Christ was defeated by evil but at the heart of this defeat, life sprang triumphant. Bernard too was defeated by evil. He experienced Gethsemani. Perhaps he needed to go that far, to be abandoned by his own: from 'you couldn't stay up with me for one hour', to the incomprehensible cry, 'Father why have you abandoned me?'

Abandonment. I didn't 'abandon' Bernard. I was faithful in my friendship. I admired his work, but I never told him so. Why?

Today I found some time for my friend — a whole afternoon. I travelled 200km for him, and without hesitation I did it for him, but he's dead. I wouldn't have travelled that far for him had he been alive. Why? Why is friendship expressed in front of a coffin and not in front of a living, breathing person who watches and waits! Crippled people who don't know how to love, to speak, to show feeling. Hearts locked in a hard shell. When will I learn to carry around a living beating heart.

And when will I learn to truly open myself to God's infinite tenderness. God who wants to reach my brothers through me; a burning love which has defeated death.

Bernard I promise you I'll go and visit the living.

With Open Heart: Michael Quoist

How Dennis Potter found serenity

Knowing for certain that he was to die within a few weeks, he said: "the only thing you know for sure is the present time. The nowness becomes so vivid to me that in a perverse sort of way I am almost serene. I can celebrate life.

"Below my window in Ross, for example, the blossom is out in full. It's a plum tree — it looks like apple blossom but it's white. And instead of saying 'oh, that's nice blossom' looking at it through the window when I am writing, it is the whitest, frothiest, blossomiest blossom that there ever could be".

What he did there, I think was to privilege those who know they have a short time to live. Such a death sentence can panic you, stupefy you, bring up the feelings of futility latent in us all. It can be seen as a wretched, weakened stump end to life sans almost everything.

No, said Potter, it can be the most compelling, the most astonishing passage of life — indeed those of us who have this knowledge of a certain end are even an elite ... "The nowness of everything is absolutely wondrous. There's no way of telling you, you have to experience it — the glory of it, if you like, the comfort of it, the reassurance."

... His words spread from the comparatively few who are ill and therefore saw not only an example of fortitude but the philosophy of positive enhanced life, to the many who have great difficulty in living in the moment; in putting aside getting and spending which "lays waste to our powers".

Dennis Potter's gift was to grace what in his and similar circumstances is largely regarded as the wasted end of a life, with a conviction and an insight, which spoke of a truth at least as great as the lengthening of a life — the truth of the quality of the lived experience. He demonstrated it in himself and articulated it for others.

At the very least, what he did for people, in the full sense of that lovely phrase, was "to give them pause".

The Times, 10th April 1996, Melvyn Bragg.

The poem was given by the author to Elizabeth Kubler-Ross, who has written the introductory paragraph.

One terminally ill patient who has made a nationwide impact is Orville Kelly — a man in his forties, full of cancer, who through his sufferings started an organisation "Make Today Count". Naturally Orville Kelly will long be remembered as the initiator of this nationwide organisation. But what we should not ever forget is that — behind all this work — all these creative innovative ideas born out of suffering and despair — is the dying man who would love to live and who knows he has to bid adieu to his loved ones. Orville's own feelings and consolation come through his own poem given to me as a gift I will always treasure.

For my wife Wanda
Love will never go away

Spring, and the land lies fresh green
Beneath a yellow sun.
We walked the land together, you and I
And never knew what future days would bring.
Will you often think of me,
When flowers burst forth each year?
When the earth begins to grow again?
Some say death is final,
But my love for you can never die.
Just as the sun warmed our hearts,
Let this love touch you some night,
When I am gone,
And loneliness comes —
Before the dawn begins to scatter
Your dreams away.
Summer, and I never knew a bird
Could sing so sweet and clear,
Until they told me I must leave you
For a while

I never knew the sky could be so deep a blue
Until I knew I could not grow old with you
But better to be loved by you,
Than to have lived a million summers.
And never known your love.
Together, let us, you and I
Remember the days and nights
For eternity.
Fall and the earth begins to die,
And leaves turn golden brown upon the trees,
Remember me, too in autumn, for I will walk with you,
As of old, along a city sidewalk at evening time,
Though I cannot hold you by the hand.

Winter, and perhaps some day there may be
Another fireplace, another room,
With crackling fire and fragrant smoke
And, turning suddenly, we will be together.
And I will hear your laughter and touch your face,
And hold you close to me again.
But until then, if loneliness should seek you out,
Some winter night when snow is falling down,
Remember though death has come to me,
Love will never go away

Death. The Final Stage of Growth:
Elizabeth Kubler-Ross.

INTO THY HANDS

"Into Thy Hands," How blessed are they who can say these words and mean them with all their hearts.

Dr. Elizabeth Kubler-Ross speaks from her vast experience of death and dying in the hospital ward. She is one of the people who have earned the right to say, as she does, "I shall be richer all my life for this sorrow." She does not belittle the sorrow, far from it, but she emphasises the support that comes from a shared sorrow. I believe we can hang on to this thought when we feel so utterly helpless in the face of unbearable sorrow. It is then that in some mysterious way which we don't understand, the very fact that someone is minding for you and sharing the sorrow with you, can help in some small way, to make the un-bearable able to be born.

We must look forward to the time when the body ceases to be and the spirit emerges free and unencumbered in its new birth.

He glories in the Lord.
I love thee, O Lord my strength
The Lord is my rock, and my fortress and my deliverer,
my God, my rock, in whom I take refuge,
my shield and the horn of my salvation, my stronghold.
I call upon the Lord, who is worthy to be praised,
and I am saved from my enemies.
He testifies to His deliverance.
The cords of death encompassed me
the torrents of perdition assailed me;
the cords of Sheol entangled me
the snares of death confronted me.

In my distress I called upon the Lord;
to my God I cried for help,
From his temple he heard my voice
and my cry to him reached his ears.

He reached from on high, he took me,
he drew me out of many waters.
He delivered me from my strong enemy,
and from those who hated me;
for they were too mighty for me
they came upon me in the day of my calamity;
but the Lord was my stay.
He brought me forth into a broad place;
he delivered me because he delighted in me.

Psalm 18

Free from the fret of mortal years,
And knowing now Thy perfect will.
With quickened sense and heightened joy
They serve Thee still.

O Fuller, sweeter is that life,
And larger, ampler is the air
Eye cannot see nor heart conceive
The glory there;

Nor know to what high purpose Thou
Dost yet employ their ripened powers,
Nor how at Thy behest they touch
This life of ours.

Source Unknown

Sharing

"I shall be richer all my life for this sorrow. New insights about life have been born. Life is to be lived by striking a line through every minus and turning it into a plus. If agony must be experienced, there are those who are ready to bear some of the burden. Where there is suffering the gift of courage is given. Courage comes from without as well as from within. The important moments in life are those shared with others, whatever the cost may be. When hurts are shared closeness is born. The gift of love is a most precious gift, and it is possible to express it most fully at the end of earthly life. I shall be richer all my life for this sorrow. New insights about death have emerged. Death is another beginning not an end. Death is a new birth into a new state. Death is not to be feared, any more than is birth. When the body ceases to be the spirit emerges, free and unencumbered. I shall be richer all my life for this sorrow.

Sorrow
It hurts deep down inside.
One feels diminished,
Less than he has been.
Empty
Bereft —
Forlorn and incomplete.
Sorrow is a painful word
But if someone is there
To share the feeling
It becomes endurable
And in the scheme of things
A time of being
That includes great emotion
And thus a time of closeness
Growing and becoming someone more
Than we have been before.

Death. The Final Stage of Growth: Elizabeth Kubler-Ross.

'Light and Life'

I thought of my first visit to Japan, that first feeling of revolt that I felt at Hiroshima, and the Lord's answer through a young girl's sensitive gesture.

I had just finished lecturing in Tokyo. Among the people who had attended and who stayed behind to ask me questions, or even wanted an autograph, a young girl came up to me. 'I live in Hiroshima' she said. 'I'm going back tonight. I came specially to thank you for your books; my friends thank you too.' With that she handed me a prettily wrapped package. I opened it. Inside was a beautiful Japanese painting. 'I did it myself' she said. The characters painted on the canvas read in Japanese, 'Light and Life'. I thanked her, but it wasn't enough. She disappeared quickly into the crowd. I don't know her name or her address. I can't even write to her. Should she ever read these lines, I want her to know that God hasn't stopped talking. It's just that now he's talking through the lives of loving people. Sometimes he speaks through the heart and paintbrush of a Japanese girl. I've only just realised it myself — thanks to her.

With Open Heart: Michael Quoist.

A Sense of Service

There will be many patients who never use the words death or dying, but they will talk about it all the time in disguised ways. A perceptive therapist can answer their questions or concerns without using the avoided words and still be of great help to such a patient.

If we ask ourselves what is so helpful or so meaningful that such a high percentage of terminally ill patients are willing to share this experience with us, we have to look at the answers they give when we ask them for the reasons for their acceptance. Many patients feel utterly hopeless, useless and unable to find any meaning in their existence at this stage. They wait for the Doctor's rounds, for an X-ray perhaps, for the nurse who brings the medication, and the days and nights seem monotonous and endless. Then into this dragging monotony a visitor comes who stirs them up, who is curious as a human being, who wonders about their reactions, their strengths, their hopes and frustrations. Someone actually pulls up a chair and sits down. Someone actually listens and does not hurry by. Someone does not talk in euphemisms but concretely, in straightforward, simple language about the very things that are uppermost in their mind — pushed down occasionally, but always coming up again.

Someone who comes who breaks the monotony, the loneliness, the purposeless agonising waiting.

Another aspect which is perhaps more important is the sense that their communications might be important, might be meaningful at least to others. There is a sense of service at a time when these patients feel that they are of no earthly use to anybody any more. As one patient put it, "I want to be of some use to somebody. Maybe by donating my eyes or my kidneys but this seems so much better, because I can do it while I am still alive".

On Death and Dying: Elizabeth Kubler-Ross.

Tormented by Waiting

There is a time in a patient's life when the pain ceases to be, the mind slips off into a dreamless state, when the need for food becomes minimal and the awareness of the environment all but disappears into darkness. This is the time when the relatives walk up and down the hospital hallways, tormented by the waiting, not knowing if they should leave to attend the living or stay to be around for the moment of death. This is the time when it is too late for words, and yet the time when relatives cry the loudest for help — with or without words. It is too late for medical interventions (and too cruel, though well meant, when they do occur), but it is also too early for a final separation from the dying. It is the hardest time for the next of kin as he either wishes to take off, to get it over with; or he desperately clings to something that he is in the process of losing forever. It is the time for the therapy of silence with the patient and availability for the relatives.

The doctor, nurse, social worker or chaplain can be of great help during these final moments if they can understand the family's conflicts at this time and help select the one person who feels most comfortable staying with the dying patient. This person then becomes in effect the patient's therapist. Those who feel too uncomfortable can be assisted by alleviating their guilt and by the assurance that someone will stay with the dying person until his death has occurred. They can then return home knowing that the patient did not die alone, yet not feeling ashamed or guilty for having avoided this moment which for many people is so difficult to face.

On Death and Dying: Elizabeth Kubler-Ross.

The Silence that goes beyond words

Those who have strength and the love to sit with a dying patient in the Silence that goes beyond words will know that this moment is neither frightening nor painful, but a peaceful cessation of the functioning of the body. Watching a peaceful death of a human being reminds us of a falling star; one of a million lights in a vast sky that flares up for a brief moment only to disappear into the endless night forever. To be a therapist for a dying patient, makes us aware of the uniqueness of each individual in this vast sea of humanity. It makes us aware of our finiteness, our limited life span. Few of us live beyond our three score and ten years and yet in that brief time most of us create and live a unique biography and weave ourselves into the fabric of human history.

"The water in a vessel is sparkling; the water in the sea is dark
The small truth has words that are clear; the great truth has great silence."

Stray Birds: Tagore.

Desolation and its Aftermath

A great deal depends on the environment around those about to make the great transition of death, whether in a concentration camp or a hospital. Those serving in hospices for the dying know the matter very well; they flow out in pure love to their patients so that nothing is too good for them. They are treated, perhaps for the first time, as people who matter in a world that is shortly to lose them to the unknown realm of death, that 'undiscovered country from whose bourn no traveller returns', to quote from Hamlet's famous soliloquy. Once an individual's self-esteem can be affirmed, a new person may break through and greet the great mystery of the afterlife with considerable conviction, especially when they are met by figures of people whom they knew earlier on in their life. In the end we grasp the full meaning of the life beyond death by personal experience in the depth of the soul. In other words, when we are quite still, the knowledge of immortality is not far from us.

Dark Victory: Martin Israel.

Death the Instructor

Thomas Mann once said: "without death there would scarcely have been poets on earth". Any person who studies poetry through the centuries can verify this. The first epic, the Babylonian Gilgamesh, and the first-known lyric poem of world literature, a poem by Sappho, dealt mainly with death. From then until now, no great poet has existed who failed to dedicate some of his most beautiful verses to death. And all of them touched the deeper secret of life while talking about death.

'No thought exists in me which death has not carved with his chisel', said Michelangelo. From the Egyptian, Etruscan, and Attic beginnings of art, modern surrealism, death has played an important part.

And as in philosophy, literature and art, death was also the great inspirer of music. The first songs were funeral dirges, and the great music of Bach, Gluck, Mozart, Beethoven, Schubert, Verdi, Mahler, Moussorgsky, and the modern composers frequently has death as its leading motif.

Death is, however, not only the inspirer of artistic imagination. It has strongly influenced the ethical attitude of human beings as well. Death was the great instructor of those noble characters in history whom we venerate as heroes, saints or martyrs of science.

Death. The Final Stage of Growth: Elizabeth Kubler-Ross.

Darkling I listened; and for many a time
I have been half in love with easeful death,
Called him soft names in many a mused rhyme,
To take into the air my quiet breath;
Now more than ever seems it rich to die,
To cease upon the midnight with no pain,
While thou art pouring forth thy soul abroad
In such an ecstasy!
Still wouldst thou sing, and I have ears in vain —
To thy high requiem become a sod.

Thou wast not born for death immortal bird
No hungry generations tread thee down;
The voice I heard this passing night was heard
In ancient days by emperor and clown:
Perhaps the self-same song that found a path
Through the sad heart of Ruth, when sick for home,
She stood in tears amid the alien corn;
The same that oft-times hath
Charmed magic casements, opening on the foam
Of perilous seas, in fairy lands forlorn

Ode To a Nightingale: John Keats.

REACHING OUT

I think one of the things which saddens me most in these days is the seemingly total lack of communication, one to one, at all levels of society. While there are more means of communication than ever before, more words from countless sources, still people are unable to speak to each other with any understanding at a deeper level than the surface of things.

We have all seen the miseries which come from this lack of understanding. In family life, between husband and wife, parents and children, between management and the shop floor, between people of different coloured skins and cultures, between those holding differing beliefs, between nations and continents.

So often this lack of communication leads to violence, war, injustices of all kinds and finally to alienation from our Creator.

There is a terrifying passage in 'I and Thou' by the Jewish mystic Martin Buber in which God says 'I have sunk my hearing in the deafness of mortals'. If this should be even partly true what a tremendous responsibility it places upon us to listen, to listen to each other with our whole attention, with our hearts, but what a difficult thing to do.

To Thee, O Lord, I call;
lest if Thou be silent to me
I become like those who go down
to the Pit.

Blessed be the Lord; for he has heard the voice
of my supplications.
The Lord is my strength and my shield
in him my heart trusts;
so I am helped and my heart exults
and with my cry I give thanks to him.
he is the saving refuge of his anointed
O save thy people, and bless thy heritage.
Be thou their shepherd and carry them forever.

Psalm 28

Part of Me

"I've seen many people die in many different ways, but I never get used to dying and death. I always feel when I meet it as if it comes for the first time, and I uncover all my heart and mind humbly before such uncomprehended royalty. This man was an utter stranger to me, but in that look he was suddenly very close, was almost part of me, if only because we are in life all near to one another in our common nearness to this end, which ultimately makes us one."

Flamingo Feather: Laurens Van der Post.

The Jewish View of Death

When the family and community are faced with the prospect of the death of one of its members, Jewish law reminds us that "a dying man is considered the same as a living man in every respect". But in American culture today dying is treated as if it were a separate realm of existence. America is essentially a death-denying society; consequently we treat the dying differently than we do the living. We avoid them or avoid honest communication with them. We try to spare them the problems of everyday living; and we therefore deprive them of its joys. The dying person lives alone in an artificial environment, created by those who do not wish to cope with the fact of death, and its inevitable call to every human being.

Hallacha forbids this dishonest approach. The dying person must be treated as he was always treated as a complete person capable of conducting his affairs and able to enter fully into human relations even unto death. Further, the Jewish tradition of never leaving the bedside of the dying is of immense value, not only to the dying person but also to those about to be bereaved. How helpless and how guilty we must feel when we hear of the death of a loved one, especially if no one was there to ease the fear of uncertainty and the pain of separation. All kinds of questions spring to mind from the well-springs of guilt, "Was everything done that could have been done?" "Why didn't the doctor or nurse get there sooner?" "What could I have done to prevent this?" "Did he suffer?" "Why was he alone" "Will I be alone?" "Will anyone care for me though I didn't care for him?" Judaism shields mourners from being overwhelmed by this kind of guilt because the community shares in the care of the dying so that they are never left alone. The community provides reassurance that everything appropriate was done. To the extent that I am part of the community, part of me was there when he died, and so I need not be afraid.

The bedside vigil serves one more purpose. As death approaches, a crisis of faith occurs as the life-cycle draws to an end. A personal confession is encouraged from the dying as a rite de passage to another phase of existence. This type of confessional occurs throughout the Jewish life cycle whenever one stage has been completed. So we confess on the Day of Atonement as we end one year of life and begin another. So brides and grooms traditionally said the confessional and fasted on their wedding day for they sensed that it marked the end of one stage in their life and the beginning of another. This, together with the recital of the Shema in the last moments before death helps to affirm faith in God precisely when it is most challenged and helps the dying person focus on those most familiar rituals of his life just at the moment he enters the most mysterious and unknowable experience of his life. This comforts him together with those who share his vigil.

Death. The Final Stage of Growth: Elizabeth Kubler-Ross.

Death and Dying

It might be helpful if more people would talk about death and dying as an intrinsic part of life just as they do not hesitate to mention when someone is expecting a baby. If this were done more often, we would not have to ask ourselves if we ought to bring up the topic with a patient, or if we should wait for the last admission. Since we are not infallible and can never be sure which is the last admission, it may be just another rationalisation which allows us to avoid the issue.

We have seen several patients who were depressed and morbidly uncommunicative until we spoke with them about the terminal stage of their illness. Their spirits were lightened, they began to eat again, and a few of them were discharged once more, much to the surprise of their families and the medical staff. I am convinced that we do more harm by avoiding the issue than by using time and timing to sit, listen and share.

I mention timing because patients are no different from the rest of us in that we have our moments when we feel like talking about more cheerful things, no matter how real or unrealistic they are. As long as the patient knows that we will take the extra time when he feels like talking, when we are able to perceive his cues, we will witness that the majority of patients wish to share their concerns with another human being and react with relief and more hope to such dialogues.

If this book serves no other purpose but to sensitise family members of terminally ill patients and hospital personnel to the implicit communications of dying patients, then it has fulfilled its task. If we as members of the helping professions can help the patient and his family to get 'in tune' to each other's needs and come to an acceptance of an unavoidable reality together, we can help to avoid much unnecessary agony and suffering on the part of the dying, and even more so on the part of the family that is left behind.

Death and Dying: Elizabeth Kubler-Ross.

In-Sight

When for you the stars sing.
And the fallen apple
Is golden green,
When you look
Into the eye of the fish
And know the pain
Of the hook,
When you share the
struggle of the seed,
And hold wet earth
In your hand with awe,
When you see the bush burn
Take off the shoes
From off your feet
For the place whereon thou standest
Is holy ground.

Reflections in a Dusty Mirror: Susan Wood.

Creative Prayer

"An encounter does not become deep and full until the two parties to it are capable of being silent together with one another. As long as we need words and actions, tangible proof, this means we have not reached the depth and fullness we seek. We have not experienced the silence which enfolds two people in common intimacy. It goes deep down, deeper than we knew we were, an inner silence where we encounter God and in God our neighbour.

In this state of silence we do not need words to feel close to our companion, to communicate with him in our deepest being, beyond ourselves to something which unites us. And when the silence is deep enough, we can begin to speak from its depths, but carefully and cautiously so as not to break it by the noisy disorder of words. Then our thought is contemplative.

Creative Prayer: Metropolitan Anthony of Sourozh.

Through Depression to Hope

When people are incurably ill, especially those facing immanent death it is very important for those around them to flow out in reasoned hope. This is not blind optimism that all will be well on this side of the grave, but a lightness of touch that seems to put the present sadness in the context of the vast universe. If matters of life and death are broached by the patient it is wiser to listen than to hold the floor with dogmatic opinions. It seems that many slowly dying patients are given deep information not only about their condition and its probable outcome, but also about those who have recently died and the preparation under way for their own transition to the life beyond physical death. The same approach is also true for those suffering from clinical depression. These often include a number of bereaved patients.

... When one's with a clinically depressed person, this communicative silence is like balm to the victim. Somehow one's deep understanding and concern are much more effectively communicated psychically from a spiritual source within one(the 'apex of the soul' where the spirit is situated, and it in turn is the focus of the Holy Spirit in each person), when one is completely silent until the Holy Spirit impels one to say a special word of encouragement or enlightenment. The apogee of communicative silence is prayer: only when we are quiet before the mystery of creation may the divine presence meet us, because then we are ready to receive God. As we grow in the way of prayer, so we begin to know that true prayer is an aware openness to the workings of God, that we may play our part in transmitting the divine love to all whom we meet in the daily round. Prayer is universal in scope, for God has no favourites. The way of communicative silence is also the most effective way of knowing God and serving our fellow creatures. Communicative silence transmits hope directly to our depressed friends and indeed all that bear the burden of misfortune and loneliness. I have little doubt that we will appreciate the silence when the body is dead and the soul passes forth into new surroundings for fresh adventures.

Dark Victory: Martin Israel.

Dark Victory

To continue giving oneself in love to a person who cannot respond is a great test of relationship. How can one continue to take a real interest in a spouse who is languishing in hospital in the last stages of Alzheimer's disease, when the rational response is so minimal that it is extremely doubtful whether the patient even recognises their visitor? One has always to be honest in one's reactions; play-acting simply increases the sense of ultimate alienation. I believe that when the brain is so damaged by the degenerative changes of Alzheimer's disease or the frank destruction of tissue that follows a stroke or an injury, the essential being of a person may be intact but unable to communicate intelligibly through an irremediably damaged brain, the master organ of the body that controls all responses while we are alive in the flesh. If one considers this possibility, one may still address the person with the hope that there is a deeper recognition even if the response is negligible.

True love embraces the entire person and looks for no response to justify it.

Dark Victory: Martin Israel.

Overwhelmed

When I feel overwhelmed by destruction.
Let me go down to the sea
Let me sit by the immeasurable ocean
And watch the surf
Beating in and running out all day and night
Let me sit by the sea
And have the bitter sea winds
Slap my cheeks with their cold damp hands
Until I am sensible again.
Let me look at the sky at night
And let the stars tell me
Of limitless horizons and unknown universes
Until I am grown calm and strong once more.

Marjorie Pizer

Death in the First Person

The author gave meaning to her life and death through her reaching out to others with a message that would carry on long after she was gone. You can further dignify her death if you will receive and act upon this message.

"I am a student nurse. I am dying. I write this to you who are and will become, nurses in the hope that by my sharing my feelings with you, you may some day be better able to help those who share my experience.

I am out of the hospital now — perhaps for a month, for six months, perhaps for a year — but no one likes to talk about such things. In fact, no one likes to talk about much at all. Nursing must be advancing but I wish it would hurry. We're being taught not to be overly cheery now, to omit the 'everything's fine' routine and we have done pretty well. But now one is left in a lonely silent void. With the protective 'fine, fine' gone, the staff is left with only their own vulnerability and fear. The dying patient is not yet seen as a person and thus cannot be communicated with as such. He is a symbol of what every human fears and what we each know, at least academically, that we too must someday face. What did they say in psychiatric nursing about meeting pathology with pathology to the detriment of both patient and nurse. And there was a lot about knowing one's own feelings before you could help another with his ... How true. But for me, fear is today and dying is now. You slip in and out of my room, give me medications and check my blood pressure. Is it because I am a student nurse myself, or just a human being that I sense your fright? And your fears enhance mine. Why are you afraid? I am the one who is dying. I know you feel insecure, don't know what to say, don't know what to do. But please believe me, if you care, you can't go wrong. Just admit that you care. That is really for what we search. We may ask for why's and wherefore's but we don't really expect answers. Don't run away — wait — all I want to know is that there will be someone to hold my hand when I need it. I am afraid. Death may get to be a routine to you but it is new to me. You may not see me as unique, but I've never died before. To me once is pretty unique. You whisper about my youth, but when one is dying, is he really so young any more? I have lots I wish we could talk about. It really would not take much more of your time because you are here quite a bit anyway. If only we could be honest, both admit our fears, touch one another. If you really care, would you lose so much of your valuable professionalism if you even cried with me? Just person to person? Then it might not be so hard to die — in a hospital — with friends close by.

Death. The Final Stage of Growth: Elizabeth Kubler-Ross.

The Fear of Death

When a patient is severely ill, he is often treated like a person with no right to an opinion. It is often someone else who makes the decision if and when and where a patient should be hospitalised. It would take so little to remember that the person has feelings, wishes, and opinions, and has, most important of all, the right to be heard.

Well our imaginary patient has now reached the emergency ward. He will be surrounded by busy nurses, orderlies, interns, residents, a lab technician perhaps who will take blood, another technician who takes the electrocardiogram. he may be moved to X-ray and he will overhear opinions of his condition and discussions and questions to members of his family. Slowly but surely he is beginning to be treated like a thing. He is no longer a person. Decisions are made often without taking his opinion. If he tries to rebel he will be sedated, and after hours of waiting and wondering whether he has the strength, he will be wheeled into the operating room or intensive treatment unit and become an object of great concern and great financial investment.

He may cry out for rest, peace, dignity, but he will get infusions, transfusions, a heart machine, or a tracheotomy. He may ask one single question, but he will get a dozen people around the clock, all busily preoccupied with his heart rate, pulse, electrocardiogram, or pulmonary functions, his secretions, or excretions, but not with him as a human being. He may wish to fight it all but it is going to be a useless fight since all this is done in the fight for his life, and if they can save his life then they can consider the person afterwards. Those who consider the person first may lose precious time to save his life! At least this seems to be the rationale or justification behind all this — or is it? Is the reason for this increasingly mechanical depersonalisation approach our own defensiveness? Is this approach our own way to cope with and repress the anxieties that a terminally or critically ill patient evokes in us? Is our concentration on equipment, on blood pressure, our desperate attempt to deny the impending end which is so frightening and discomforting to us that we displace all our knowledge on to machines, since they are less close to us than the suffering face of another human being which would remind us once more of our lack of omnipotence, our own limitations and fallibility and last but not least perhaps our own mortality?

Maybe the question has to be raised: Are we becoming less human or more human? This is no way meant to be judgemental but it is clear that whatever the answer may be the patient is suffering more — not physically, perhaps, but emotionally. And his needs have not changed over the centuries, only our capacity to gratify them.

On Death and Dying: Elizabeth Kubler-Ross.

MANY MANSIONS

I read somewhere of a nurse in a large hospital serving many ethnic patients, who organised a group of people with the aim of enquiring into the needs of the dying and seriously ill patients who belonged to other faiths than Christianity.

She was aware that in their different cultures so many were having to die without the spiritual help and consolation provided by their particular religions. Thus giving them added suffering in their loneliness and separation from their beliefs.

I do hope that she succeeded in her most perceptive caring for the spiritual needs of her patients.

The Lighting of the Memorial Candles

We light six candles in memory of the six million Jews — men, women and children — who were systematically murdered in the heart of our so-called civilized Christian word. We light a seventh in memory of the countless others who were murdered by the Nazis. As we light these candles, we commit ourselves to responsibility for one another, to build on this earth a world that has no room for hatred, no place for violence. Together we pray for the strength to fulfil this vocation.

****

At the end of our time of prayer, we say together:

We remember the six million Jewish men and women, one million children among them, who were murdered when madness ruled the world and evil dwelt on earth. We remember all those others who were caught in the eddies and swirls of the Shoah.

We mourn for all those that died with them — their goodness and their wisdom, which could have saved the world and healed so many wounds. We mourn for the genius and wit that died, the learning and the laughter that were lost. The world has become a poorer place and our hearts become cold as we think of the splendour that might have been.

We stand in gratitude for their example of decency and goodness. They are like candles which shine out from the darkness of those years. We salute these men and women who were not Jews, who had the courage to stand outside the mob and suffer with the Jewish community. We honour the rescuers.

May such times never come again. May such sacrifice never be in vain. In our daily fight against cruelty and prejudice, against tyranny and persecution, their memory gives us strength and leads us on.

In silence we remember those who sanctified God's name on earth. Amen

Holocaust Memorial Day with the Sisters of Sion

True Peace

Wherever I go in the West, I am struck by the great mental suffering that arises from the fear of dying, whether or not this fear is acknowledged. How reassuring it would be for people if they knew that when they lay dying they would be cared for with loving insight! As it is, our culture is so heartless in its expediency and its denial of any real spiritual value that people when faced with terminal illness feel terrified that they are simply going to be thrown away like useless goods. In Tibet it was a natural response to pray for the dying and to give them spiritual care. In the West the only spiritual attention that the majority pay to the dying is to go to their funeral!

At the moment of their greatest vulnerability then, people in our world are abandoned and left almost totally without support or insight. This is a tragic and humiliating state of affairs which must change. All of the modern world's pretensions to power and success will ring hollow until everyone can die in this culture with some measure of true peace, and until at least some effort is made to ensure this is possible.

The Tibetan Book of Living and Dying: Sogyal Rinpoche.

Spiritual Help for the Dying

I first came to the West at the beginning of the 1970s, and what disturbed me deeply, and has continued to disturb me, is the almost complete lack of spiritual help for the dying that exists in modern culture. In Tibet, as I have shown, everyone had some knowledge of the higher truths of Buddhism and some relationship with a master. No one died without being cared for, in both superficial and profound ways, by the community. I have been told many stories of people dying alone and in great distress and disillusion in the West without any spiritual help, and one of my main motivations in writing this book is to extend the healing wisdom of the world I was brought up in, to all men and women. Do we not all have a right, as we are dying, not only to have our bodies treated with respect, but also and perhaps even more important, our spirits? Shouldn't one of the main rights of any civilised society, extended to everyone in that society, be the right to die surrounded by the best spiritual care? Can we really call ourselves a "civilisation" until this becomes an accepted norm? What does it really mean to have the technology to send people to the moon, when we do not know how to help our fellow humans with dignity and hope?

Spiritual care is not a luxury for the few; it is the essential right of every human being, as essential as political liberty, medical assistance and equality of opportunity.

A real democratic ideal would include knowledgeable spiritual care for everyone as one of its most essential truths.

The Tibetan Book of Living and Dying: Sogyal Rinpoche.

Forgiveness

I would like to single out two points in giving spiritual help to the dying: giving hope and finding forgiveness.

Always when you are with a dying person, dwell on what they have accomplished and what they have done well. Help them to feel as constructive and as happy as possible about their lives. Concentrate on their virtues and not on their failings. People who are dying are frequently extremely vulnerable to guilt, regret and depression; allow the person to express these freely, listen to the person and acknowledge what he or she says. At the same time, where appropriate, be sure to remind the person of his or her buddha nature, and encourage the person to try to rest in the nature of mind through the practice of meditation. Especially remind the person that pain and suffering are not the all that he or she is. Find the most skilful and sensitive way possible to inspire the person and give him or her hope. So rather than dwelling on his or her mistakes, the person can die in a more peaceful state of mind.

To the man who cried out "Do you think God will ever forgive me for my sins", I would say "Forgiveness already exists in the nature of God, it is already there. God has already forgiven you, for God is forgiveness itself. To err is human and to forgive divine'. But can you forgive yourself? that's the real question.

Your feeling of being unforgiven and unforgivable is what makes you suffer so.. But it only exists in your heart and mind. Haven't you read how in some of the near-death experiences a great golden presence of light arrives that is all-forgiving? and it is very often said that it is finally we who judge ourselves.

The Tibetan Book of Living and Dying: Sogyal Rinpoche.

The Feast of the Dead

One of the very difficult things that Europeans have to learn to understand about Japan is the extreme seriousness with which death is treated. In Japan it is not treated as something which is purely an end or purely negative. It is something for which one needs almost as much preparation, ceremonial, devotion and love as for marriage.

I have always been deeply stirred by the great Feast of the Dead — Japan's All Saints Day — when everyday life stops and minds and houses are opened wide to welcome the dead. This is one of the most joyful acts of remembrance I have ever encountered.

A Walk With a White Bushman: Laurens Van der Post.

Who Dies?

In this culture we look at life as if it were a straight line. The longer the line the more we imagine we have lived, the wholer we suppose ourselves to be, and the less horrendous we imagine the end point. The death of the young is seen as tragic and shakes the faith of many. But in the American Indian culture one is not seen linearly but rather as a circle which becomes complete at about puberty with the rites of passage. From that time on one is seen as a wholeness that continues to expand outward. But once the "hoop" has formed, any time one dies, one dies in wholeness. As the American Indian sage, Crazy Horse, commented, "Today is a good day to die for all the things of my life are present". In the American Indian wisdom wholeness is not seen as the duration one has lived but rather the fullness with which one enters each complete moment.

Unlike culture which encourages little preparation for death, in the American Indian culture at the time of death a naturally formed crystal is often offered for use as a meditation object. Gazing into the fissures within the crystal that create prismatic rainbow lines one projects one's consciousness into the rainbow, letting go of all that keeps the mind from focusing beyond itself. At death one is guided into the rainbow body, melting out of temporal form with ease and wise preparation.

There seems to be much less suffering for those who live life in the wholeness that includes death. Not a morbid preoccupation with death but rather a staying in the loving present, a life that focuses on each present moment. I see few whose participation in life has prepared them for death. Few who have explored their heart and mind for whatever might come next be it death or sickness, grief or joy.

Who is prepared to die? Who has lived so fully that they are not threatened by their imaginings of nonexistence? For it is

only the idea of death that frightens us. It is the unknown we
pull back from.

*An Investigation of Conscious Living
and Conscious Dying*: Stephen Levine.

Sun Bear on the Native American way of dying

In the old way, when it was time to die old ones would go off by themselves feeling that the moment of death was as intimate between them and The Earth Mother as the moment of birth is between human mother and child. They would find a quiet place and there make prayers to the Great Spirit, thanking him for the life they had enjoyed. They would sing their song and they would die.

… Like all other things in life, death is not permanent. It is but a change from one world, from one state of being into another. For those of us who learn to love life, with all its changes, death should not be a fearful event. It should be a time of celebrating the continual evolution of the soul. When it is your time to pass, it should be with your mind wide open and your prayer in your heart. When one dear to you dies, besides sadness at your loss you should feel happiness that now the soul is free to soar to Kitche Manitou, the Great Spirit, our common Creator. Where there is love there is no room for fear.

Unwanted

It has been said that 'we die alone', but there are degrees of loneliness, and the feeling of being unwanted at the end of life may be the most poignant of all human emotions.

I have come more to realise that it is being unwanted that is the worst disease that any human being can ever experience. For all kinds of diseases there are medicines and cures. But for being unwanted, unless there are willing hands to serve, and a loving heart to love, I don't think this terrible disease can ever be cured.

Mother Teresa of Calcutta

BEYOND THE BLUE MOUNTAINS

I was once asked to speak about bereavement. I think I was invited because I had experienced the two kinds of bereavement that so many of us have lived through. The shock of a sudden and unexpected death and the long drawn out agony of seeing a much loved person dying slowly.

First of all I want to emphasise that in any comment relating to the bereavement of others, one cannot, must not generalise. We are all different, we all react in our different ways. The circumstances of death are so varied. For some it comes as a sudden and terrible shock, for others it is a long drawn-out anguish. But there are three aspects which I think apply in every case.

The first and possibly the most important is acceptance The second is the offering of our sorrow to God   The third is the sense of guilt.

Perhaps I might say a few words about each of these aspects. First, acceptance, and by acceptance I don't mean resignation which I think of as negative, but acceptance as a positive, creative reaction. Something has happened which cannot be altered which has changed every minute of the 24 hours of every day. Something with which we have to learn to live. Until this is accepted we cannot start to live our lives again and life must go on, however different it will be.

We must be given time to mourn, to adjust to this total change, time to grieve for the one we have lost. Our friends must be patient and stand by us. Words cannot really help much but it does help that friends understand and are concerned for us

Offering. Any offering of our sorrow, our pain, our loneliness, even of any anger and bitterness, to God who understands and comforts and upholds us through our misery. I believe that to offer all to God repeatedly is the best thing we can do, perhaps the only thing we can do. This may not bring us consolation at once, but the knowledge that our offering will be heard and accepted will gradually bring us inner peace, the peace of God which passes all understanding, the peace we have been promised.

The third, possibly the most difficult, subject to talk about is the sense of guilt. Some of us have to face this and to come to terms with it. I don't believe there are many people who do not suffer in this way when they lose someone close to them. What mistakes did I make? How much I regret some of the things I have said, done, or left undone. Why did I not make it plain how much I loved them. One could go on for ever. I think this is a reaction which has to be conquered. It is totally negative and does not help anyone. Perhaps we have to accept that we have made mistakes, ask for forgiveness and know that even if we find it hard to forgive ourselves we have, by the mercy of God received forgiveness.

The Lord my Shepherd

The Lord is my shepherd, I shall not want
  he makes me lie down in green pastures.
He leads me beside still waters;
he restores my soul.
He leads me in paths of righteousness
for his name's sake.

Even though I walk through the valley of the shadow of
death
I fear no evil;
for thou art with me;
thy rod and thy staff,
they comfort me.
He is host to his people for ever.

Thou preparest a table before me
in the presence of my enemies;
thou anointest my head with oil,
my cup overflows.
Surely goodness and mercy shall follow me
all the days of my life
and I shall dwell in the house of the Lord
for ever

Psalm 23

Here is a poem which I think says everything I would want to say about acceptance.

Acceptance

He said I will forget the dying faces
The empty places
They shall be filled again;
O voices mourning deep within me cease
Vain, vain the word, vain
Not in forgetting lieth peace.

He said I will crowd action upon action
The strife of my faction
Shall stir my spirit to flame;
O tears that drown the fire of manhood cease
Vain, vain the word, vain, vain
Not in endeavour lieth peace.

He said I will withdraw me and be quiet
Why meddle in earth's riot
Shut be my door to pain
Desire thou dost befool me; thou shalt cease
Vain, vain the word, vain, vain
Not in aloofness lieth peace.

He said, "I will submit; I am defeated
God hath depleted
My rich life its gain,
O futile murmurings; why will ye not cease?"
Vain, vain the words, vain, vain
Not in submission lieth peace.

He said "I will accept the breaking sorrow
Which God tomorrow
Will to his son explain",
Then did the turmoil deep within him cease,
Not vain, the word, not vain
For in acceptance lieth peace.

Amy Carmichael

God for Nothing

Perhaps humility recognises that there is nothing you can do for a bereaved person; you are useless and empty. But you can *BE* with her, wait with her, pay attention to her, as she confronts the night and the storm. The role of the servant is to wait on her, not to tell her what to do. 'Welcome. Rest here. Here is space and silence'. But how painful it is to remain silent when we long to rush in with advice and answers. Humbly we wait on someone, to pay attention to her often means silence and a sort of withdrawal — you intrude as little of yourself as you can in order to leave as much space as possible for her to explore her feelings. You have no answers; only she has the answers, and, if she is given enough space and attention, then she may be able to hear the call to her journey that is sounding through her pain. Really to listen is so costly; it makes us feel helpless and passive, the ear being the feminine part of the body, the opening through which people come to us. If we talk enough then our ears will be closed to them. And there is another point of contact — our own wounds, the places where our protective skin of self-assurance has been pierced. Perhaps because we have been wounded ourselves, we are able to meet others more directly. To freeze and join the living dead, to try to retreat or run away, to adopt unrealistic temporary escape routes, these are all ways in which we react to crisis. But to have the courage to seek one's own creative solution — then the suffering is not all in vain and perhaps new life lies ahead. It is costly for the listener and costly for the one who is listened to — God knows how costly, but God is in the space, and the wound, and God is in the voice that calls through the wound. And God can cope with failure.

God for Nothing: Richard MacKenna.

The Infinite Universe of the Resurrection

When someone we love dies and when we experience their dying we return to our own living with a clearer and purer perception of the true perspective of life simply because we have participated in the death of one we love — in a death of part of ourselves. And death itself, especially the death of someone we have loved teaches us what love teaches us. It reveals to us that the more deeply we love and enter into communion, so the more radically we must become detached and non-possessive. To continue to fall in love we must continue to fall away from the ego. It is the final and most demanding of the lessons life teaches us. It is the meaning of the absolute finality of the Cross, the single-pointedness of the Cross that yet opens up into the infinite universe of the Resurrection.

Death the Inner Journey: John Main.

Love — and Gratitude

The agony is so great
And yet I will stand it.
Had I not loved so very much
I would not hurt so much.
But goodness knows I would not
Want to diminish that precious love
By one fraction of an ounce.
I will hurt,
And I will be grateful to the hurt
For it bears witness to the depth of our meanings,
And for that I will be
Eternally grateful.

> *Death The Final Stage of Growth*: Elizabeth Kubler-Ross.

Change

Albert Einstein wrote:

"Day and daily we come up against dying and grieving. The people we work with or bump into. Therefore our understanding of death and grief are of paramount importance. It is only when we ourselves come to terms with our own concept of dying and death by carefully thinking it through, searching our minds for our true feelings and thoughts on the subject can we go forward and help others through that most trying time. We all at some stage of life go through a 'little death'. Some are more significant than others but together help us to grow, help our feelings to mature and help us to learn what life is all about with all its ups and downs. We must learn to let go, to go forward without something or someone we love and want very much.

Life is full of change — from birth onwards we meet these 'little deaths' — when a toy is taken from us, when we are denied something we want, when we leave home and go to school, to college, get married and set up a new life which in itself will start with a new set of 'little deaths'. Hurt and disappointment in the marriage, with the children — all have the same reaction in one way or another — anger, sadness, loneliness, helplessness, shock, self-reproach, these plus others are all reactions to death — the grief process. By coming through we will be able at the end to cope with the ultimate death.

Joy and woe are woven fine,
A clothing for the soul divine,
Under every grief and pine,
Runs a joy with silken twine.
It is right it should be so,
Man was made for joy and woe,
And when this we rightly know,
 Through the world we safely go.

William Blake.

Death the Inner Journey

Meditation, as I have suggested, is a way of dying and a way of living. While you are saying the mantra you are dying to what is the most difficult thing in the world to die to. We die to our own egoism, to our own self-centredness as we go beyond our own self-consciousness. And the reason is simply that while you are saying the mantra you are not thinking about yourself. You are attending to the mantra. And as through a lifetime you learn to say the mantra with deeper and deeper abandonment, with stronger and stronger faith, you die to everything that restrains you from the fullness of life. It is this fullness of life that is our destiny. As Jesus put it I have come that you may have life, life in all its fullness. As we die to the ego we rise to a way of life that astonishes us with its infinite richness, its wonder and above all with its absolute liberty of spirit. Meditation is a healing process. What is healed is the essential wound we all have: The wound of the divided self that separates us from ourselves, from others, from God — and so from our own full potential.

... The only way to prepare for death is to die day by day. This is the spiritual journey even before it is a religious one. Religion is the sacred expression of the spiritual but if the spiritual experience is lacking, then the religious form becomes hollow and superficial and self-important. Religion does yield high dividends, but only to the man whose resources are within him.

The way of meditation is a personal way. Dying is a personal journey. No one can meditate for us and no one can die for us. So many barriers and fears come down as a person faces death. So much more freedom is gained to put out our hand to another. And it is the same with meditation.

John Main.

The Gift of Our Being

I think it would be important for anyone introducing a spiritual dimension into the therapeutic situation to be aware that there has to be a distinction between prayer as petition and prayer as an entry into the reality of the situation: into Reality itself. When we meditate we accept the gift of our own being, and if our being happens to be full of joy and light at that moment we accept that. If our being happens to be facing the trauma of death we accept that. It is the acceptance of our own being, as we are, at this moment in our life's journey. That is what meditation is about. It is not trying to regain control over life, not trying to change God's mind, not trying to change our fate or destiny, not trying to reinstate the threatened ego as managing director of our personality. Meditation leads to an acceptance of the reality of the human situation as it is here and now.

A Short Span of Days: Laurence Freeman.

Birth and Death

Death blessings were known as 'soul leading' or 'soul peace'. A soul-friend, the 'anam-chara' almost always a lay person, would sing or intone the soul-peace over the dying person, and all present would join in beseeching the three persons of the Godhead and all the saints of Heaven to receive the departing soul. During the prayer the soul-friend would make the sign of the cross with the right thumb over the lips of the dying. It was an occasion which drew from Andrew Carmichael some of his more colourful prose.

"The scene is touching and striking in the extreme and the man or woman is not to be envied who could witness unmoved the distress of the lovable people of the West taking leave of those who are near and dear to them in their pilgrimage, as they say, of crossing the black river of death, the great ocean of darkness; and the mountains of eternity. The scene may be in a lowly cot begrimed with smoke and black with age, but the heart in not less warm, the tear not less bitter, and the parting not less distressful than in the court of the noble or the palace of royalty".

He was also moved by an account of a funeral at which 'I am going home with thee' was sung — characteristically to the air of a secular song. He spoke to people who had heard it in Lewis. They said that the scene and the tune were singularly impressive — the moaning of the sea, the mourning of the women, and the lament of the bagpipes over all as the body was carried to its home of winter, to its home of autumn, of spring and summer; never could they forget the solemnity of the occasion, where all was so natural and so beautiful and nature seemed to join in the feelings of humanity.'

I am going home with thee.
I am going home with thee
To thy home; to thy home!

I am going home with thee
To thy home of winter.

I am going home with thee
  To thy home, to thy home!
I am going home with thee
To thy home of autumn, spring and of summer.

I am going home with thee,
Thou child of my love,
To thine eternal bed,
To thy perpetual sleep.

I am going home with thee
Thou child of my love,
To the dear Son of blessings.
To the Father of grace.

The Celtic Vision: Esther de Waal.

Fruit Gathering

Let me not pray to be sheltered from
dangers but to be fearless in facing them
Let me not beg for the stilling of
my pain but for the heart to conquer it
Let me not look for allies in life's
battlefield but to my own strength,
Let me not crave in anxious fear to
be saved but hope for the patience to
win my freedom.

Grant me that I may not be a coward,
feeling your mercy in my success alone;
but let me find the grasp
of your hand in my failure.

Rabindranath Tagore

Attention

Attention doesn't mean rushing around or trying to impose your own solutions or telling people to go on holiday, join a prayer group, pull themselves together, trust God, take up a hobby. Attention means waiting with someone, being with them accompanying them. Only they can follow the path set before them — no one else can do it for them — but to know that there is someone there who takes them utterly seriously, who is within call, and who has perhaps done their share of wrestling through the night — all this gives courage to go on and to grow. The astonishing thing about so many letters to the problem page was that people would write back thanking you for advice, helpful contacts and so on. But most of all they would just want to say thank you for taking them seriously and for letting them know that they mattered, that they were important. So often there was no answer to give to a problem, but the fact that someone had listened, had paid attention to them, without trying to lessen the pain or draw a veil over it, seemed to give them strength to go on, more confident to be themselves.

God for Nothing: Richard MacKenna.

Presence

The person in misery does not need a look that
judges and criticises
but a comforting presence
that brings peace and hope and life
and says
"You are a human person," is important
mysterious
infinitely precious
what you have to say
is important
because it flows
from a human person
in you there are those seeds
of the infinite
those germs of love … of beauty
which must rise from the earth
of your misery
so humanity be fulfilled.
if you do not rise
then something will be missing
if you are not fulfilled
it is terrible
you must rise again
on the third day …
rise again because we all need
you
for you are a child of God
you, sam
john
willie, mae
my brother … my sister
be loved
beloved.

Tears of Silence: Jean Vanier

Soul Making

Tears soften the soul, clear the mind and open the heart. Weeping has a triple function. It softens the hardened and dried out soul, making it receptive and alive. It clears the mind. It opens the heart ... You should grieve for the sake of the God who grieved for you. This says something startling about the kind of God to whom the believer owes allegiance, a God who grieves, who weeps, who suffers.

Dietrich Bonhoeffer the Lutheran Pastor in his letters from prison in his poem 'Christians and Pagans' talks about God in His hour of grieving.

> Men go to God when they are sore bestead
> Pray to him for succour for his peace, for bread
> For mercy for them, sick, sinning or dead.
> All men do, Christian and unbelieving
>
> Men go to God when they are sore bestead
> Find him poor and scorned without shelter or bread,
> Whelmed under weight of the wicked, the weak, the dead,
> Christians stand by God in his hour of grieving.
>
> God goes to every man when sore bestead.
> Feeds body and spirit with his bread,
> For Christians, pagans alike he hangs dead.
> And both alike forgiving.

Soul Making. What inspires compassion is the love we have for one another. Compunction is the means by which we begin to love our neighbour. It is related to the Kingdom which is God's plan for healing creation. All things are held in being by the mercy and love of God and the gift of tears helps us to see just that. What saves it from becoming a burden too grievous to be borne is that it reflects us from being attached to our own ends, goals and schemes and leads us into the heart of God. There we can see that the pursuit of our own perfection is as ludicrous as it is impossible. In the heart of God is our heart's desire and nothing less than God will satisfy us ... Let everyone bring tears. Even the poorest of us can at least bring tears, they have the power of resurrection.

Compassion

"he who has been
deeply hurt
has a RIGHT
to be sure
he is
LOVED

Love
not just some passing moment
a glance however open
but some deeper compassion
radiating permanency
not some morbid curiosity
some gushing pity
incompetent naivete

the cry of burnt-out eyes
wounded bodies
afflicted minds
cravings
can only be answered by some deeper love
in which is felt a strange presence of the eternal
a hope
a new security
not some passing glance
but deeper bonds
unbreakable

com-passion
is a meaningful word ...
the same suffering
the same agony
accepting in my heart
the misery in yours, o, my brother
and you accepting me.

o yes there is fear
but even more deeply
there is the insistent cry from the entrails of the
suffering one
that calls me forth …
some faint feeling
of confidence
that my smile … my presence
has value and can give
life.
thus deep friendship is born
mutual presence
humble and forgiving
engendering quiet joy, fidelity

Tears of Silence: Jean Vanier.

Recovering

Kindness, concern,
words, said with care
are stitching together
what is aching and sore
and living sources awaken
sharing in the renewed
strength of faith
kindling hope
waiting for love
to enter.

Requiem: Margrit Dahn.

The Crucible of Suffering

Something happened in life which "knocked the bottom out of things" — an unexpected sorrow, a bereavement with all its heartache, a moral tragedy in the family circle, a collapse of the economic foundations of our life. In some such way our faith was cast into the crucible and submitted to the searing heat of the flames. One was not aware at the time that one's faith had been cast into the melting pot. It was enough that one was able to struggle on and keep going with the externals of life.

It was only afterwards that when one tried to resume the old familiar associations and activities with one's fellows, that one became aware that a mysterious change had taken place in the depth of one's being. It was just not possible to pick up again one's tracks at the point at which one had come to a sudden stand still. The faith once so stoutly defended and propagated in the face of sceptic and unbeliever, not only failed to speak to our condition; it was just not there! There was, strangely enough, neither belief nor unbelief. The only response of which one was capable was akin to that of Job when he exclaimed: "but now after I have suffered, I abhor myself and repent in dust and ashes". What does this mean if it be not that from henceforth, in deep humility, one will only be able to keep a profound silence until ... we know not what? There will no longer by any easy speeches, and if one should dare to venture in among the councils of the wise, it would be to take a back seat, with a vague but perhaps wistful hope that one might hear something that might speak to one's condition.

This state of mind might prevail for some considerable time, extending not merely for a few months, but possibly into several years. This crucible will need time to cool before its contents can be investigated. But when that time comes, what shall we find? Probably something very different from our former faith. It will be very much reduced in content. It will probably be something scarcely recognisable as a faith in the former meaning of the word. Things which were once considered to be fundamental will now no longer be there. They will have been vaporised away. They were part of the former compound and not the basic element. So we shall not feel we have been deprived of anything essential. On the contrary we shall feel that we are confronted with real fundamentals, for our very being will have been laid bare to the mystery of our own personal existence. As we start to rethink our way through things our starting point will have to be this basic elemental experience. The distinction will have been forced upon us, between the things which we recognise as valid and the things which are untestable assumptions. The former alone will now count for us, and if the time ever comes when we try to help others these alone will be the cutting edge of conviction. The words we use may be feeble, hesitant and inadequate; at times we may even be constrained to use a new language which sounds very foreign to that of the old orthodoxy. But something will surely get through. The pure element, refined by the flames of suffering, will be recognised for what it is, because heart will speak to heart, the only valid language for the occasion. And in our thinking we shall not so much be asking questions and looking for adequate answers as waiting for the dawning of new understanding. Perhaps it will be to learn what is meant by the proverb; "The fear of the Lord is the beginning of wisdom, and the knowledge of the holy is understanding".

The Crucible of Suffering: Ronald Blackburn.

One cannot fail to recognise the special anguish of bereavement as the result of someone's suicide. The strongest stabs of self-reproach can be unrelenting, and ripples of remorse seem to spread very widely even affecting mere acquaintances.

I do not know the circumstances of this poem but those who are suffering greatly after a suicide could perhaps hang on to the thoughts in it.

The Existence of Love

I had thought that your death
Was a waste and a destruction,
A pain of grief hardly to be endured.
I am only beginning to learn
That your life was a gift and a growing
And a loving left with me.
The desperation of death
Destroyed the existence of love,
But the fact of death
Cannot destroy what has been given.
I am learning to look at your life again
Instead of your death and your departing.

Marjorie Pizer

Strong in Love

Here on the quiet summit we find as we have seen already, not a truth merely but a Person. Strong in His personal love and willingness rich with His unspeakably personal experience. He is able to be touched with the feeling of our infirmities' and our wounds. He is able to 'save, to the uttermost', from all their weariness and their heavy loads, those who will let Him have His way. He is able with personal methods of His own, to transfigure sorrows into joys. Consider HIM. Let it sink always deeper into your torn and tired spirit that such a person exists — living, loving, accessible. He is 'there at the Gate' whom readers of the *Pilgrim's Progress* will remember, 'Here is a poor burthened sinner', said the Pilgrim, 'I would know, Sir, if You are willing to let me in'. 'Here', let us say, 'are stricken and broken hearts; we have heard, Sir, that Your heart was once broken, and has stood open ever since, and that a great rift is turned into a gate by which men go in and find peace. We would know if You are willing to let us in'.

'I am willing with all my heart', said the Man and with that he opened the Gate.

A Search for Meaning in Suffering: H.C.G. Moule.

PARTING THE FIBRES

Parting the Fibres

One of the hardest things to come to terms with when growing old is the feeling that we are no longer of use to anybody.

In fact we can hardly avoid becoming a burden and a responsibility for the people we love.

We have to get used to the idea that we are now on the receiving end, to be helped rather than being the helper.

This is hard but it is essential.

I hope that some of the quotations in this section will underline the ways in which we, the aged and retired people, can still make our contribution.

We can still listen. Jesus has so much to say about listening and seeing, having our ears and eyes open to others for others.

We can still be there for anyone who needs an ear to listen, a shoulder to cry on, a friend to care.

So few people have time to listen, to really listen. This takes time and time is one of the commodities we are given when we are old.

We can still give thanks for all the joys we have experienced in this life, and our acceptance of it's sorrows.

For our hopes for the life to come.

Henri Nouwen quotes Christ's words "It is good for you that I go ... because if I go I can send the Spirit to you. Henri Nouwen suggests that we too can send the spirit by offering to those we love 'a new bond' He may be speaking of the next world but perhaps we may be enabled to do this in our remaining days here on earth.

Prayer

After immense Activity one passes into a phase where passivity is the only way. I pray that you may be finding this passivity as the way in which the soul serves God, not by doing this or that but by passively receiving the great stream of His love and compassion.

Michael Ramsey.

Acts of Remembrance

And some there be, which have no memorial; who are perished, as though they had never been born; and their children after them.

But these were merciful men, whose righteousness hath not been forgotten.

Their bodies are buried in peace; but their name liveth for ever more.

The people will tell of their wisdom and the congregation will shew forth their praise.

Sending the Spirit

Few words of Jesus have affected me personally so much as his words about his own approaching death. With great directness Jesus speaks to his closest friends about the end. Although he acknowledges the sorrow and sadness it will bring, he continues to announce his death as something good; something full of blessing full of promise, full of hope. Shortly before his death he says "Now I am going to the one who sent me, not one of you asks me, 'Where are you going?' Yet you are sad at heart because I have told you this. Still I am telling you the truth: it is for your own good that I am going, because unless I go, the Spirit will not come to you: if I go, I will send him, to you. I shall have many things to say to you, but they would be too much for you to bear now. However, when the Spirit of Truth comes he will lead you to the complete truth, since he will not be speaking of his own accord, but will say only what he has been told; and he will reveal to you the things to come" (John 16:4-7, 13).

At first these words may sound strange and unfamiliar and even far away from our daily struggle with life and death, but after my conversation with many friends facing death, Jesus's words strike me in a new way and express the deepest significance of what they are experiencing. We may be inclined to look at the way Jesus prepared himself and his friends for his death as unique, far beyond our own 'normal' human way. But in fact Jesus's way of dying offers us a very hopeful example. We, also, can say to our friends; 'It is for your own good that I am going because if I go I can send the Spirit to you and the Spirit will reveal to you the things to come' … Isn't sending the Spirit the best expression for not leaving those you love alone but offering them a new bond, deeper than the bond that existed in life? Doesn't dying for others mean dying so that others can continue strengthened by the Spirit of our love?

Our Greatest Gift. A Meditation on Dying and Caring: Henri Nouwen.

Wounded Healers

I met him on the train,
and before long, I felt I knew him
I felt I could trust him
He was in education; 'Learning for Life' he called it.
I said I was interested in education too,
so he invited me to come with him
to where he taught and learned.
It was off the main road, near the fire station.
It didn't look like a school ...
You walked in the door of a second hand shop,
and going through the back,
you came to a big room, with a lot of people in it,
We stood and looked around.
(pause).
In the corner was an old man with a white stick
Beside him sat a girl reading him the newspaper.
'Nice to see young folk helping the blind' I said.
'Oh' he replied 'he's actually teaching her how to see.

Across the floor in the direction of the toilets, came a wheel
chair.
A palsied boy of 18 sat in it and a boy the same age pushed
it.
'It's great when friends help each other', I said.
'Yes' he replied 'the boy in the chair is teaching the other
how to walk.

An old woman lay in a bed at the bottom of the room.
She was covered with open sores.
A woman much her junior was bathing her and dressing
her
wounds.
'Is she a nurse'? I asked
'Yes' he replied 'the old woman is a nurse.
She's teaching the other how to care'.

Seated round a table were a group of young couples.

A doctor in a white coat was talking to them about childbirth.
He spoke slowly and used sign language with his hands.
'I think it is only fair that deaf people should know
about these things' I said.
'But they do know about these things' my friend replied,
They are teaching the Doctor how to listen'.

And then I saw a woman on a respirator, breathing slowly.
These were her last breaths.
And around her were her friends soothing her brow,
holding her hands,
'It's not good to die alone' I said.
'That's right' he replied,
But she is not dying alone.
She is teaching the others how to live'.
Confused and not knowing what to say,
I suggested we sat down.

After a while, I felt I could speak.
Seeing all this, I said 'I want to pray,
I want to thank God that I have all my faculties.
I now realise how much I can do to help'.

Before I could say more, he looked me straight in the face
and said
'I don't want to upset your devotional life,
But I hope you will also pray
To know your own need, and not to be afraid to be touched
by the needy.

Trevor Nash.

If you cut a tree at its roots, you condemn it to death.
If you dry up the source, you eliminate the river.
If you cut yourself off from Christ, you die.
By wanting to eliminate God from their lives, people take
on the responsibility of humanity's suicide.

With Open Heart: Michael Quoist.

The Fibres of My Being

When the signs of age begin to mark my body (and still more when they touch my mind), when the ill that is to diminish me or carry me off strikes from without or is born within me; when the painful moment comes in which I suddenly awaken to the fact that I am ill or growing old; and above all at the last moment when I feel I am losing hold of myself and am absolutely passive in the hands of the great unknown forces that have formed me; in all those dark moments, O God, grant that I may understand that it is you (provided only my faith is strong enough) who are painfully parting the fibres of my being in order to penetrate to the marrow of my substance and bear me away within thyself.

The Divine Milieu: Pierre Teilhard de Chardin.

Man's life is laid in the lock of time
To a pattern he does not see,
While the Weaver works and the shuttles fly
Till the doom of eternity.

Some shuttles are filled with silver thread
And some with threads of gold.
While often but the darker hue
Is all that they may hold.

But the weaver watches with skilful eye
Each shuttle fly to and fro
And sees the pattern so deftly wrought
As the loom works slow and sure.

God surely planned that pattern,
Each thread — the dark and the fair —
Was chosen by His master skill
And placed in the web with care.

He only knows the beauty
And guides the shuttles which hold
The threads so unattractive
As well as the threads of gold.

Not till the loom is silent
And the shuttles cease to fly
Shall God unroll the pattern
And explain the reason why.

The dark threads are as needful
In the Weaver's skilful hand
As the threads of gold and silver
In the pattern that He has planned.

Author Unknown.

A Return to Love

We came here to co-create with God by extending love. Life spent with any other purpose in mind is meaningless, contrary to our nature, and ultimately painful. It's as though we've been lost in a dark, parallel universe where things are loved more than people. We over-value what we perceive with our physical senses, and under-value what we know to be true in our hearts.

Love isn't seen with the physical eyes or heard with the physical ears. The physical senses can't perceive it; it's only perceived through another kind of vision. Metaphysicians call it the Third Eye, esoteric Christians call it the vision of the Holy Spirit, and others call it the Higher Self. Regardless of what it's called, love requires a different kind of "seeing" than we're used to — a different kind of knowing and thinking. Love is the intuitive knowledge of our hearts. It's a "world beyond" that we all secretly long for. An ancient memory of this love haunts all of us all the time, and beckons us to return.

Love isn't material. It's energy. It's the feeling in a room, a situation, a person. Money can't buy it. Sex doesn't guarantee it. It has nothing at all to do with the physical world, but it can be expressed nonetheless. We experience it as kindness, giving, mercy, compassion, peace, joy, acceptance, non-judgement, joining and intimacy. ... Love is within us. It cannot be destroyed, but can only be hidden. The world we knew as children is still buried within our minds

A Return to Love: Marianne Williamson.

With Open Heart

The day the happiness of others becomes yours,
The day the suffering of others becomes yours,
    You may say that you love.
But it's hard to love — it hurts so much.

With Open Heart: Michael Quoist.

Old Age

These are the surest days
The Freest,
These are the oldest days,
The Dimming,
These are the youngest days
For new life is springing.
New sight beginning
As I sit pensively
In the shadow
Of the rock-fall.

Death is the assimilation of the self into the dimension of the spirit and the divine. This is why it frightens us, loss of self is so unimaginable. Yes our spirits have made that journey before in communication with God through prayer and meditation. By developing the life of the spirit we shall develop antennae to recognise that shore and feel at home in that country of the divine.

Pain, illness, and all the attributes of death are to help us shed our attachment to our bodies, and to ourselves. As they diminish, the spaces are filled with the Spirit, with God. The glimpses we get of that dimension help us on the last earthly journey.

It is the loss of self that is most daunting, and which the churches do all they can to fill the feeling of the void. In all religions and all mythology the dragons of that world turn out to be the messengers of God.

Reflections in a Dusty Mirror: Susan Wood.

Looking Forward

There will come a time, O Lord
when my links with earth grow weaker
when my powers fail
When I must bid farewell to dear ones
still rooted in this life
with their tasks to fulfil
and their loved ones to care for
When I must detach myself
from the loveliest things
and begin the lonely journey.

Then I shall hear the voice
of my beloved Christ, saying
"It is I, be not afraid".

So with my hand in his
from seeming dark valley
I shall see the shining City
and climb with trusting steps
and be met
by the Father of souls
and clasped in the everlasting arms.

George Appleton.

The Mysterious Journey

Death begins the day we are born, Living is a series of deaths and births. Those who don't accept death refuse life.

Psychologists know this, and they teach people how best to live the stages between the first birth and the last death, or to put it in another way, the various 'deaths' of our existence: childhood must die for adolescence to be born and adolescence must give way to adulthood.

And when old age is upon us, we must prepare for the mysterious journey which does not lead to another life but to the other life.

Jesus said that he who clings to his life loses it; he who accepts losing it, finds it.

With Open Heart: Michael Quoist.

Union

St. Thomas Aquinas, commenting on our Lord's cry to the Father says, "God withdrew his protection but did not break the union".

There will be times in the life of almost all of us when it seems that God has withdrawn his protection. It is then we need to trust, to have faith, that he has not broken the union. And we need to go on in that faith, in that trust, in that understanding.

"That's what Jesus did".

Eric James.

Markings

We die the day when our lives cease to be illuminated by the steady radiance renewed daily, of a wonder, the source of which is beyond reason.

Markings: Dag Hammerskjøld.

Tao Te Ching

Know the strength of man
But keep a woman's care!
Be the stream of the universe!
Being the stream of the universe
Ever true and unswerving,
Become as a little child once more.

Know the white
But keep the black!
Be an example to the world!
Being an example to the world,
Ever true and unwavering,
Return to the infinite

Know honour
Yet keep humility
Be the valley of the universe!
Being the valley of the universe,
Ever true and resourceful
Return to the state of the uncarved block.

When the block is carved it becomes useful
When the sage uses it, he becomes the ruler
Thus a great tailor cuts little
Do you think you can take over the universe
and improve it
I do not believe it can be done.
The universe is sacred
You cannot improve it
If you try to change it
If you try to hold it, you will lose it.

So sometimes things are ahead
sometimes they are behind
Sometimes breathing is hard, and
sometimes it comes easily:
Sometimes there is strength

and sometimes weakness
Sometimes one is up and sometimes down.

Therefore the sage avoids extremes
excesses and complacency.

Lao-Tzu.

The Blessings

Then he showed me the river of the water of life, bright as crystal, flowing from the throne of God and of the Lamb, through the middle of the street of the city; also on either side of the river, the tree of life with its twelve kinds of fruit, yielding its fruit each month; and the leaves of the tree were for the healing of the nations.

There shall no more be anything accursed, but the throne of God and of the Lamb shall be in it, and his servants shall worship him; they shall see his face, and his name shall be on their foreheads. And night shall be no more; they need no light of lamp or sun, for the Lord God will be their light and they shall reign for ever and ever.

Revelation 22: 1-5

Timidity: sculpture by Naomi Blake.

PART II

Dying We Live

BEYOND THE HORIZON

For the second half of this anthology I have included extracts from the writings of people who have experienced death but have remained in touch with their friends still living on this earth.

If Jesus had meant us to know more about the hereafter, would he not have left us with more details of what to expect? Perhaps we are not meant to know exactly what it will be like, but it seems wise to consider the matter and to prepare ourselves as well as we can.

So often the messages that have come through to some of us have seemed so very trivial and unimportant and unrevealing. However, two people I have chosen to quote, the late Frances Banks MA, formerly Sister Frances Mary of the Community of the Resurrection, Grahamstown South Africa, and General Lord Rawlinson, both seem to me to have given us constructive intimations of a future life.

They give us advice on the way to prepare ourselves for the next world and also report on the work they are continuing to undertake and the people they have met. Their messages seem to me to have the 'ring of truth'. In my own case I know of three authentic reports of near death experiences. The first came from my grandmother who 'died' and was resuscitated. Her second son, my godfather, who was my hero had been killed at Suvla Bay in that disastrous campaign in Gallipoli early in the First World War. When last seen he was lying wounded in the blazing grass, which had been set on fire by the shelling.

My grandmother said that when she died 'Gerald was there to welcome me'

The second example of a near death experience comes from my youngest sister who had been given too much gas when having a tooth extracted. She remembered the feeling 'this is what I have been waiting for all my life', it was a wonderful experience for her, but I suspect that there was panic in the surgery!

The third incident concerned my eldest sister's gardener, who *told her that he had 'died' and been brought back to life and would never again be afraid of dying.*

The Appearance to Mary of Magdala

Meanwhile Mary stayed outside near the tomb, weeping. Then still weeping she stopped to look inside, and saw two angels in white sitting where the body of Jesus had been, one at the head and the other at the feet. They said "Woman why are you weeping?" 'They have taken my Lord away' she replied 'and I do not know where they have put him'.

As she said this she turned round and saw Jesus standing there, though she did not recognise him. Jesus said "Woman why are you weeping? Who are you looking for? Supposing him to be the gardener, she said 'Sir, if you have taken him away, tell me where you have put him and I will go and remove him' Jesus said 'Mary'. She knew him then and said to him in Hebrew, 'Rabbuni!' — which means Master. Jesus said to her 'Do not cling to me, because I have not yet ascended to my Father, but go and find the brothers and tell them: I am ascending to my Father and your Father, to my God and your God'. So Mary of Magdala went and told the disciples that she had seen the Lord and that he had said these things to her.

John: 20

Prayer

Father
If the hour has come
to make the break,
help me not to cling,
even though it feels like death
Give me the inward strength
of my Redeemer Jesus Christ;
to lay down this bit of life
and let it go,
so that I and others may be free
to take up whatever new and fuller life
you have prepared for us,
now and hereafter.
Amen.

John V. Taylor.

Mister God This is Anna

On our homeward journey from church Anna practised her newly discovered game with me. In the same manner that she launched her spiritual being at Mister God, so she launched her physical being at me.

With her remarks she hurled herself at Mister God and he caught her. Anna knew that he would, knew that there was no risk involved. There was really no other way, it just had to be done. This was her way of being saved.

Her game with me was similar. She would stand some distance off, run towards me and launch herself at me. The run towards me was deliberate and active, the moment after her launch she was completely passive and limp. She made no effort to help me catch her, no effort towards her own safety. Being safe meant not doing these things at all, being saved meant trust in another.

Every minute of every day Anna lived, she totally accepted her life and in accepting life, accepted death. Death was a fairly frequent topic of conversation with Anna — never morbid or anxious, simply something that would happen at some time or other, and it was better to have some grasp of it before it happened than to wait until the moment of death and then get panicky about it. For Anna death was the gateway to possibilities.

Fynn.

Trust the Catcher

I would like to tell a story about 'the Flying Rodleighs'. They are Trapeze artists who perform in the German Circus. When I first saw the Rodleighs move through the air, flying and catching I will never forget how enraptured I became.

One day I was sitting with Rodleigh, the leader of the troupe, in his caravan talking about flying. He said 'As a flyer I must have complete trust in my catcher. You and the public might think that I am the great star of the trapeze, but the real star is Joe, my catcher. He has to be there for me with split-second precision and grab me out of the air as I come to him in the long jump'. 'How does it work?' I asked. 'Well' Rodleigh said, 'the secret is that the flyer does nothing and the catcher everything! When I fly to Joe, I have simply to stretch out my arms and hands waiting for him to catch me and pull me safely over the apron behind the catchbar'. 'You do nothing!' I said quite surprised. 'Nothing', Rodleigh repeated. 'The worst thing the flyer can do is to try to catch the catcher. I am not supposed to catch Joe. It's Joe's task to catch me. If I grabbed Joe's wrists, I might break them, or he might break mine and that would be the end for both of us! A flyer has to fly and a catcher has to catch and the flyer has to trust, with outstretched arms, that his catcher will be there for him.'

When Rodleigh said this with so much conviction the words of Jesus flashed through my mind: 'Father into your hands I commend my spirit.' Dying is trusting in the Catcher! Caring for the dying is saying 'Don't be afraid, remember you are the beloved Son of God. He will be there when you make your long jump ... don't try to grab him, he will grab you. Just stretch out your arms and hands and trust, trust, trust.

*Our Greatest Gift. A Meditation on
Dying and Caring*: Henri J.M. Nouwen.

Ted Hughes writes to me:

"Here is a copy of my selected poems. Since you know how I read them perhaps they will not baffle you, as they baffle many. I try to write as I talk — but perhaps more concentrated.

Most readers are looking for something else — and of course cannot imagine the invisible musical score which is simply my particular way of talking. If I had recited any, I would have given you New Foal (page 235) and Anniversary (291), Miriam was my Mother's sister who died early — then visited her throughout her life, gradually turning into a very tall angel made of flames. My brother was much older than me — a sort of extra Father.

Anniversary.

"My mother in her feathers of flame
Grows taller. Every May Thirteenth
I see her with her sister Miriam. I lift
The torn-off diary page where my brother jotted
'Ma died today' — and there they are
She is now as tall as Miriam.
In the perpetual Sunday morning
Of everlasting, they are strolling together
Listening to the larks
Ringing in their orbits. The work of the cosmos,
Creation and destruction of matter
And of anti-matter
Pulses and flares, shudders and fades
Like the Northern Lights in their feathers.

My mother is telling Miriam
About her life which was mine, Her voice comes, piping,
Down a deep gorge of woodland echoes:
'This is the water-line, dark on my dress, look.

Where I dragged him from the reservoir.
And that is the horse on which I galloped
Through the brick wall
And out over the heather simply
To bring him a new pen. This is the pen
I laid on the altar, and these
Are the mass marriages of him and his brother
where I was not once a guest. 'Then suddenly
She is scattering the red coals with her fingers
To find where I had fallen
For the third time she laughs.

Helplessly till she weeps.
Miriam who died at eighteen
Is Madonna-like with pure wonder
To hear all she missed. Now my mother
Shows her the rosary prayers of unending worry
Like pairs of shoes, or one dress after another,
This is the sort of thing she is saying,
I like to wear best. And: much of it,
You know was simply sitting at the window
Watching the horizon. Truly
Wonderful it was, day after day,
Knowing they were somewhere. It still is.
Look.

And they pause, on the brink
Of the starry dew. They are looking at me.
My mother, darker with her life.
Her Red Indian hair, her skin
So strangely olive and other-wordly,
Miriam sheer flame beside her.
Their feathers throb softly iridescent
My mother's face is glistening
As she held it into the skyline wind
Looking towards me. I do this for her.

She is using me to tune finer
Her weeping love for my brother, through mine,
As if I were the shadow cast by his approach.

As when I came a mile over fields and walls

Towards her and found her weeping for him —
Able for all that distance to think me him.

A Time To Die

The faith that God's loving care keeps those who go trustfully through the gate of death, and that the crucified Christ Jesus is present with those who bear the burden of sorrow, can and does bring light and healing to broken spirits.

One question remains: "Shall we meet again and know each other after death?" It could well be asked by the parents of that child killed by the lorry, or by the husband of Constance, the young wife who has by now gone from him; and by the father of the young nurse who died and by anybody at any time struck down this way. William Barclay was himself one of them, for he lost a young daughter in a drowning accident. That fact gives him a special right to this question, and is a justification for quoting him … 'There is the constantly recurring question whether we shall know and meet and recognise each other on the other side of death. One thing is quite certain. Christian orthodoxy does not teach the immortality of the soul; it teaches the resurrection of the body. We do not mean by that the resurrection of the body as it is … We would never wish for the resurrection of a body with which a man had been smashed up in an accident or died with an incurable disease. It so happens that Greek has no work for personality; and the resurrection of the body means the survival of the personality: It means that "In the life beyond you will still be you, and I will still be I".

A Time to Die: William Purcell.

Unseen Helpers

The last words one of my sisters spoke to me as she lay dying were, "I am sure I shall be allowed to help you from the other side. "All I can say is that someone unseen has continually helped me, not least when I have been trying to write a letter, an article, or a sermon or a book to help others. To what extent a sermon is partly made on the "other side" it is impossible to say. And why is one so consciously "guided" at times to make a visit, to write a letter or to send a book? Who sent that woman last night fifty miles to ask me a question the answer to which set her mind at rest? Why did that particular man make that particular journey to attend that particular service at which all unknown to him beforehand, his particular problem was dealt with:

I must not enlarge on this, but again and again I have suddenly written down the name of one of my people and felt I had to visit his home, only to find that he was in some special need. Again and again, while preaching I have altered the sermon or an illustration in it, only to find that the alteration was relevant to the need of a previously unknown listener. My own solution of the mystery is that unknown friends in the unseen, who see "with larger, other eyes than ours", convey to one the need they see.

The Christian Agnostic: Leslie Weatherhead.

The Mists of Avalon.

Avalon is a magical island that is hidden behind huge impenetrable mists. Unless the mists part, there is no way to navigate your way to the island. But unless you believe the island is there, the mists won't part.

Avalon symbolises a world beyond the world we see with our physical eyes. It represents a miraculous sense of things, the enchanted realm that we knew as children. Our childlike self is the deepest level of our being.

It is who we really are and what is real does not go away. The truth does not stop being the truth just because we're not looking at it. Love merely becomes clouded over, or surrounded by mental mists.

Avalon is the world we knew when we were still connected to our softness, our innocence, our spirit. It's actually the same world we see now, but informed by love, interpreted gently, with hope and faith and a sense of wonder. It's easily retrieved, because perception is a choice. The mists part when we believe that Avalon is behind them.

And that's what a miracle is: a parting of the mists, a shift in perception, a return to love.

A Return to Love: Marianne Williamson.

The dirge of death

Thou goest home this night to thy home of winter
To thy home of autumn, of spring, and of summer;
Thou goest home this night to thy perpetual home;
To thine eternal bed, to thine eternal slumber.

Sleep thou, sleep and away with thy sorrow
Sleep, thou sleep and away with thy sorrow;
Sleep thou beloved in the rock of the fold.

Sleep this night in the breast of thy Mother,
Sleep thou beloved, while she herself soothes thee;
Sleep thou this night on the Virgin's arm,
Sleep thou this night, while she herself kisses thee.

The great sleep of Jesus, the surpassing sleep of Jesus
The sleep of Jesus' wound, the sleep of Jesus' grief,
The young sleep of Jesus, the restoring sleep of Jesus,
The sleep of the kiss of Jesus of peace and of glory.

The Celtic Vision: Esther De Waal.

A NEW CREATION

I have sometimes been worried by the question of whether or not the people who have died, and whom we love, are still concerned about their friends and relations on earth. Do they worry about us as we go through the traumas of life, experiencing disasters and sorrows of all kinds? The following extracts go some way towards relieving my anxiety.

That very day two of them were going to a village named Emmaus, about seven miles from Jerusalem, and talking with each other about all these things that had happened. While they were talking and discussing together, Jesus himself drew near and went with them. "What is this conversation which you are holding with each other as you walk?" And they stood still looking sad. Then one of them named Cleopas, answered him. "Are you the only visitor to Jerusalem who does not know the things that have happened there in these days?" And he said to them "What things?" And they said to him, "Concerning Jesus of Nazareth who was a prophet mighty in deed and word before God and all the people, and how our chief priests and rulers delivered him up to be condemned to death, and crucified him. But we had hoped that he was the one to redeem Israel. Yes and besides all this it is now the third day since this happened. Moreover, some women of our company amazed us. They were at the tomb early in the morning and did not find his body; and they came back saying that they had even seen a vision of angels who said that he was alive. Some of those who were with us went to the tomb and found it just as the women had said, but him they did not see". And he said to them, "O foolish men, and slow of heart to believe all that the prophets have spoken! Was it not necessary that the Christ should suffer these things and enter into his glory?" And beginning with Moses and all the prophets he interpreted to them in all the scriptures the things concerning himself.

So they drew near to the village to which they were going. He appeared to be going further but they constrained him saying "Stay with us, for it is toward evening and the day is now far spent". So he went in to stay with them. When he was at table with them, he took the bread and blessed and broke it, and gave it to them. And their eyes were opened and they recognised him and he vanished out of their sight. They said to each other, "Did not our hearts burn within us while he talked to us on the road, while he opened to us the scriptures?" And they rose that same hour and returned to Jerusalem and they found the eleven gathered together and those who were with them who said, "The Lord has risen indeed, and has appeared to Simon!" Then they told what had happened on the road, and how he was known to them in the breaking of bread.

Luke 24: 13–25

Resurrection: Life through Death

"The resurrection stories are trying to describe the "New Creation" in language of the old creation. The very words have to be transformed by the inner reality of this marriage of heaven and earth. What "really" happened is no longer what human eyes could see in a four-dimensional universe. The words are describing the new reality in which things on earth and things in heaven are woven together into a new context ... I came to the edge of this mystery when my first wife died, and though I have told the story before, I must tell it again, knowing that many people can tell similar stories from their own experience. She had had an operation for cancer some months before, when her pituitary gland was removed. "I feel I have lost my horse", she said — my energy, my spirit. A week or so after her death my children and I went on holiday to Anglesey and were walking round the cliffs at Rhoscolyn where I have been almost every year of my life. We came over a rise and saw in front of us a horse two fields away, in a place where I have never seen a horse before or since. It raised its head, whinnied, and came galloping through a gap in the wall and across these two fields to meet us at the stile we were just about to cross. It was a mare in foal and she licked our hands. I knew with that inner clarity which comes through the experience of death, that in and through that real horse, my wife, my children's mother, had come back to us. She was saying, "Look, I've got my horse back! I am so happy you are on holiday, and I am with you". This was both an objective and subjective experience. From the other side of death somebody has taken an initiative. The real presence of my wife had come to us in the body of a real horse. She had spoken to us through a symbol which to those who loved her was charged with the meaning of her death and resurrection.

The Dance of Love: Stephen Verney.

Dr. Patricia Graeme who sent this poem to me has devoted much of her life to caring for those dying of cancer.

She is one of the people who can speak with the true authority which comes from experience of the needs, the fears, the hopes of those who are about to die.

The poem had been sent to Dr. Graeme anonymously from the Canary Islands and arrived through her letter box during the time when her husband was dying of cancer.

"Do you need me?
I am there
You cannot see Me, yet I am the light you see by
You cannot hear Me, I speak through your voice.
You cannot feel Me, yet I am the power at work in your hands
I am at work though you do not understand My ways
I am at work though you do not recognise My works.
I am not strange visions. I am not mysteries.
Only in absolute stillness beyond self can you know Me as I am,
and then but as a feeling and a faith.
Yet I am there, Yet I hear, Yet I answer.
When you need Me I am there.
Even if you deny Me, I am there.
Even when you feel most alone, I am there.
Even in your fears, I am there
Even in your pain I am there,
I am there when you pray and when you do not pray.
I am in you and you are in Me.
Only in your mind can you feel separation from Me, for only in your mind are the mists of "yours" and "mine".
Yet only with your mind can you know Me and experience Me.
Empty your heart of empty fears
When you get yourself out of the way, I am there
You can of yourself do nothing, but I can do all,
And I am in all.
Though you may not see the good, good is there, for I am there.
I am there because I have to be, because I am

Only in Me does the world have meaning, only out of Me does
the world take form, only because of Me does the
world go forward.
I am the law on which the movement of the stars and the
growth of living cells are founded.
I am the love that is the law's fulfilling, I am assurance
I am peace, I am oneness, I am the law that you can live by.
I am the love that you can cling to.
I am your assurance, I am your peace. I am one with you,
I am.
Though you fail to find Me, I do not fail you.
Though your faith in Me is unsure, My faith in you never
wavers, because I know you, because I love you
Beloved I am there.

Author Unknown.

Prayer and the Pursuit of Happiness

The Christian Faith gives us the conviction that through the death and resurrection of Christ one day the sun of happiness will rise and never set. It is possible to have a deep optimism about life that despite the tragic dimension, the values we cherish will shine out triumphantly, that the purpose of divine love will prevail. This gives us the freedom to receive ordinary human happiness, when it comes without desperately pursuing it at all costs.

Prayer and The Pursuit of Happiness: Richard Harries.

So gentle was His coming
no voice
no opening door
nor step upon the stair
but a quiet peace of presence
He was there
No fear
No dread alarm
only a tender calm
Divine down stooping
gathering up
mortality
fulfilment
like a brimmed cup.

Anonymous

The Eternal Now

A promise sure to be fulfilled in the after-life must be that of fellowship. Those who really love will be drawn to one another even though their spiritual and mental achievements and stature may be very different. Jesus promised to be with a dying revolutionary with whom He could have had little in common. At the same time a merely conventional relationship even though it be of husband and wife, surely cannot force people to be together. Most of us if we are honest, would rather find fellowship with close friends than with difficult relatives. For myself I would rather spend eternity with a horse I knew in the desert of Mesopotamia than with a church official I knew in England. indeed if we have truly loved an animal we may have endowed it with a survival power. Everything that can be said here is bound to be speculative. We do not know why the animal creation exists, or what purpose its creation achieves but within the so-called group-soul the beloved animal may continue to exist awaiting its redemption or perhaps its reincarnation into some higher expression of life — perhaps as part of its owner's life.

The Christian Agnostic: Leslie Weatherhead.

So This is Death

Thus life is vanquished by mortality,
And faith without hope dies ... And yet there stands,
If Christ be true, God's crowned Charity

On the still frontier of the timeless lands,
Whence death is outlawed, to receive and guide
The homeward soul with his own piercéd hands.

For the Great Potter cannot cast aside
The treasurers of his fond and patient art,
So dear that of his charity he died

Even he, for their sake, of a broken heart
And knew himself the bondage of the tomb
Before he rent the bands of death apart.

In one of many mansions there is room
(Though falls to dust Thy leasehold tenement)
Prepared for thee. Now from the kindly womb

Of death shall spring thy new embodiment,
Wrought in a mould more rare than this poor clay.
Death's conqueror forbids me to lament

This muddled outworn vesture of decay:
Fold the thin hands and close the blinded eyes,
Windows to thy dear soul but yesterday,

And write upon the gravestone thus: 'Here lies
The dust untenanted, by mortal breath,
Of one who woke to see in Paradise

The Face of Charity. Yea, this is death

So This is Death: G.A.G. Bowden.

The Greatest Adventure

Death still remains the greatest of man's adventures.

To be able to embark on it in the same spirit of wonder as a child sets out on his holiday by the sea, is what we must all wish for ourselves and those we love.

The greatest of all death's functions in man's restless consciousness is that it unifies for him as nothing else can — not even love — the whole vast and diverse universe of time and space. It makes him a citizen of all worlds and all ages: above all, of all that he has ever loved, to all eternity. Only in his own silence can a man hear the music of the spheres.

From *Arthur Bryant's Biography*

The Testimony of Light

As you know from my life story, I dedicated myself to the religious life and after years of repeating these creeds and forms with my lips, years during which my will was stretched and exerted to keep me honourably performing to the best of my ability those vows which I had so solemnly made, after twenty-five years of such devotion to my religion I found myself unable to go on any longer.

Not that I no longer believed in God, or did not care to follow the pattern of Jesus, nor that I doubted that Christ was the Light of the World, but because, into my experience and thoughts had seeped to me a new explanation of these mysteries. Personal discovery had implanted within me doubts of the veracity of those tenets of the faith which even more than twenty years ago were being superseded as outmoded, limited in interpretation, and impractical forms of modern belief.

Now, in this new world to which I am gradually being introduced with all its beauty and light and freedom, I can look back with joy that such a step was part of my experience. For I have not, like so many good and conventional souls, arrived here with thought and expectation coloured by old half-truths; with prejudices against survival of the personality as well as of the soul to be dissolved, albeit painfully, in this new expression of freedom. At least I am thankful to relate, I can in expectation, in anticipation, in utter belief of a new life, and thus I found joy in the reunion of old contacts as well as delight in the Law of recompense and of service. I passed through the experience of death firmly believing in the Resurrection, but not of the body that clothed me on earth. How could I ever desire to bring an old worn-out thing into this new life? Or ever to occupy it again with any future experience.

Here I have a body, certainly, but it is of finer composition than my late physical body. Here I look as I did on earth, or relatively as I looked, but here I am free to refashion this body by thought. I am beginning that adventure of breaking out of the prison of those creeds which limited the reality of life. Here I dwell temporarily amongst my fellow religious in a community which is entirely dedicated to helping souls awaken to a grater freedom before they proceed onwards to their 'rightful places', and to the extent in which I am allowed to participate, I am learning more and more of the true values of each soul's experience in all the worlds through which it is destined to pass in its progress toward Divinity.

The Testimony of Light: Helen Greaves.

The Divine Pattern

There are no tenets, no creeds, no formulae, no hard and fast rules devised by any mind to restrict or confine progress here. All is individual, and yet all is for the good of the whole; for the advancement of the group. It is a "forward and backward" movement, if I may be allowed to use a contradictory expression. Each soul and each group moves onward towards greater expansion, towards the divine conception of an illimitable Creation, individually and collectively. Yet at the same time each group and each soul directs 'backward' to the plan below, its present achievement, the fruits of its knowledge. These ideas, ideals and conceptions fit into and make manifest the Divine Pattern or Plan as far as this can be accepted by the souls still steeped in the illusion and glamour of matter. No acceptance of another soul's belief colours progress. The soul must judge for itself — must make its own progress, must choose what to accept as truth for itself. No soul is coerced, forced or bound by creeds. If he believes that this is Heaven, or conversely, that he is in Hell then for him that is so at his present state of progress.

Helpers and Teachers and Great Souls there are in number to explain such errors of thinking, but there are no rules to follow and obey except the Divine Precept of Love, Light, Wisdom and Understanding.

The Testimony of Light: Helen Greaves.

The Nazi Leader

Our 'patient' is still 'sleeping'. He has not changed and will possibly continue to rest in this pure Light of healing and love until his soul has regained sufficient strength and peace to begin his long progress onwards.

I have talked with the Jewish girl who arrived with him. She has recovered sufficiently to begin to re-orient her thought; to change the angle of her thinking. She was a 'good' woman, that is she was moral and kind and loving but it will take much instruction and gentle working out of her problems before she will be enabled to view the horror of what happened to her in an objective manner. The old ingrained 'eye for an eye' and 'tooth for a tooth' belief has to be transmuted through this new angle of judging into an appreciation of Love as the instigator of life. Already some of the virulent hatred is dissolving as she now realises that the avenger receives nothing constructive or worthwhile by insisting on recompense.

Mother Florence told her about the poor soul who was the instigator of her tragedies, and she knows that he is even now resting, and being 'healed'. So far she can scarcely bear to think of his being healed, but she will. Now all that she asks is to be reunited with the husband and child who were taken from her. Her own sufferings in the camp to which she was taken and where she later died, are being obliterated in her consciousness as she is learning to relax and let go of the earthly life and all the terror and hate in it and to live in the Light.

Her husband, who was a German lawyer, was 'rounded up' and transported to a labour camp where he too, later died from injuries and exposures. She never knew what happened to her little girl. Mother Florence tells me that the husband has been 'located'. He did not hold the hatred in his soul so deeply or so bitterly and has progressed more easily. He has awaited the arrival of the wife he loved and has continually sent her Love and Light, even whilst she was sojourning in those shadowy worlds of the lower astral bound by the hate bonds to the man who had caused the tragedies. Perhaps it was the very fact of that Light sent down to her and to the soul of the man who was responsible for the cruelties, which helped to set them free from the underworld, so that Messengers could bring them here. In the nature of consciousness (which is the way here of saying 'in the fullness of time') he will come to meet her. They will be reunited and will go their way together.

The Testimony of Light: Helen Greaves.

As torrents in summer
Half -dried in their channels,
Suddenly rise, tho' the
Sky is still cloudless,
For rain has been falling.
Far off at their fountains.

So hearts that are fainting
Grow full to o'erflowing
And they that behold it
Marvel, and know not
That god at their fountains
Far off has been raining.

Saga of King Olaf: Henry Wadsworth Longfellow.

The Following messages from the other side of death come from General Lord Rawlinson. In the foreword to the second edition Mr. Rawlinson his nephew writes.

"These messages have come from time to time through the hand of one who is no professional medium and had never experienced anything of the kind before.

"I give them to all who will read them in full assurance that they will bring hope and happiness".

The General died in India and a friend of mine who had served under him was deputed to bring his body home by sea.

He told me that the messages came through the General's secretary who had never previously acted as a medium. They came in his own handwriting and in just the way he would have phrased them.

They were published first in 1926 and were reprinted 11 times till the second edition appeared in 1935.

The Awakening

My life has been very happy ever since the time I awoke from the sleep that came after the pain was over. The sleep did not last very long, but it changed everything and I had no more body and it was so difficult to believe one could be the same person without a body, but I very soon began to understand how to do things in the new life.

It is because so many people long to come to their loved ones and cannot, and because so many people believe that there is no real life after what we have always called death, that I want you to give these messages to all the world who cares to read them. You are sure to be able to convince, at all events a few people that it really is me.

My time has been fearfully occupied and I am in no way cut off from the work which I was doing. I am so glad to be able to help many who are finding things difficult. It is not possible for me to remove difficulties but I can help people to get over them by telling them how to meet them. We are all meant to have difficulties but we can get through by exercising those powers which are given to us from God by the spirit that is in us.

Revelation: General Lord Rawlinson.

Army Life

"The life of an officer in the Army is tremendously responsible. From the day he joins, the youngest subaltern has the lives of the men under his command and always under the influence of his example.

We used to think that so many of the thoughtless things we did as young men were very often fine and splendid and that we had a right to be superior to other people. I myself was one of the wilder, but I know now that if I had not done many of the things that I did it would have been better for other people.

... War is perhaps one of the things that brings us in contact with real life and real death more than anything else. We have to spend the whole of our time in contact with other people and see them on active service with all their disguises removed and just as they truly are. It is not possible for me now to state my views about war because I have changed all that since I cam here. We do change when we get further insight. I say to you all to work for peace, for only thus can the world be saved from the abomination of desolation, but meanwhile from the point of view of life on earth and a profession, one can get nearer to God, perhaps in the army than any other way, if we live our lives well and thoughtfully simply because it brings us nearer to our fellow men and gives us the opportunity of knowing them, working for them, loving them and doing all in our power to uplift the thought of the world on to a very high plane.

... Here I only want to tell you things about war from a moral standard, and I will just say that whereas the last great war was the most tremendous disaster in history and one came right up against hell in the trenches, yet one also came up against heaven. You heard so much about the horrors of it, because naturally the material outcome was the uppermost in people's understanding, but there was the other side, and great and glorious were the deeds, the thoughts and the experiences on the spiritual side.

It was wonderful to know that amongst the clash and clangour of the war one could at moments retire into the inner shrine of one's ideas and live so close to God even for a few seconds at a time.

Revelation. Letters from The Other Side of Death.
General Lord Rawlinson.

How to be in Touch

"We can so often come to you when you are alone and quiet ... We want you to know how we can best come to you, because then if you want us you will put yourselves in the position to receive what we are so wanting to give. First of all in the Communion if you go to it with your mind attuned to believe in the Communion of Saints we can be closer to you than anywhere else. The altar has been the meeting place all down the ages and will go on being so as long as the world endures because it is in the heart of mortal man and its glorious tradition has created an atmosphere that only eternity can do away with.

It will be so wonderful when we all meet in the Great Beyond at the spiritual altar with all races and kindreds and rogues gathered in all through the centuries.

... Then in your loves and friendships we are very close to you. We can see so deeply into your loving hearts just as your reproachful and bitter hearts shut us out. You have no idea how much we rejoice in your loves. Human love, whether of husband and wife, mother and child, brother and sister, friend and friend is the thing that we can share and help you with more than anything else. Be so sweet and loving to all who you know, it helps so in the working of the world.

Revelation. Letters from the Other Side of Death:
General Lord Rawlinson.

SONGS OF THE REDEEMED

Thomas, called the Twin, who was one of the Twelve, was not with them when Jesus came. When the disciples said 'We have seen the Lord', he answered. "Unless I see the holes they made, and unless I can put my hand into his side, I refuse to believe".

Eight days later the disciples were in the house again and Thomas was with them. The doors were closed, but Jesus came in and stood among them. 'Peace be with you' he said. Then he spoke to Thomas. 'Put your finger here; look, here are my hands. Give me your hand. Put it into my side. Doubt no longer but believe'.

Thomas replied, 'My Lord and My God!' Jesus said to him 'You believe because you see me.

Happy are those who have not seen me and yet believe'.

John 20: 24–29

Everlasting Fruitfulness

When we listen deeply to Jesus's words we come to realize that we are called to live like him, to die like him and to rise like him because the Spirit — the Divine Love, who makes Jesus one with his Father — has been given to us. And so, not only the death of Jesus, but our death too, is destined to be good for others. And further that, not only the death of Jesus, but our death too, will bring the Spirit of God to those we leave behind. Yes, the great mystery is that all people who have lived with and in the spirit of God, participate through their death, in the sending of the Spirit. Thus, God's Spirit of love continues to be sent to us and reveals how Jesus' death continues to bear fruit through all whose death is like his death, a death for others.

In this way, dying becomes the way to an everlasting fruitfulness. We touch here the most hope-giving aspect of death. Our death may be the end of our productivity, or fame or our importance among people, but it is not the end of our fruitfulness. The opposite is true; the fruitfulness of our lives shows itself in its fullness only after we have died. We remain too preoccupied with our accomplishments and have no eye for the fruitfulness of what we live. But the beauty of life is that it bears fruit long after life itself has come to an end: Jesus says, "In all truth I tell you, unless a wheat grain falls into the ground, it remains only a single grain, but if it dies, it yields a rich harvest'. (John 12:24).

Our Greatest Gift. A Meditation on Dying and Caring: Henri J.M Nouwen.

Judgement and Hell

If by the phrase "the day of judgement" we mean an experience after death, when, free from the physical body we first contemplate reality with a clearer and more immediate sense of a divine encounter, then it may truly be said that for thousands of people who have thought little of themselves and dreaded death and its "afterwards" (after death, the judgement), the day of judgement will be the happiest day they have ever known. For the first time, perhaps, they will be completely understood. Compassionate omniscience will know the hard, steep path they have trodden, the alluring power of the temptations of the flesh, now put aside, the hidden impulses of good, the secret longings for holiness, the brave silences and the hidden pain. They will find themselves believed in for the first time, in a way that releases them finally from the bondage of past sins and the exaggerated guilt-feeling which has tied them down for so long. With new life and belief in themselves, free from anxiety and worry, they will mount up with wings as eagles and begin a new life with all the old fears and dreads and anxieties behind them and remembered only as one remembers a bad dream.

All this, of course, does not make light of sin or take away all meaning from the word 'translated "hell". How are we to understand this word and its use in the Gospel?'

No words used in the Gospels can legitimately be twisted to mean unending punishment, and indeed, such an expression is self-contradictory. The main motive of punishment surely is to reform the sufferer; in school, to make a better scholar; in the State, to make a better citizen. If the punishment goes on for ever when does the sufferer benefit by the punishment or use the lessons he had learned so painfully? If hell were endless it would be valueless.

But God will never desert the soul. Let me add the quotation from Browning ...

that sad, obscure, sequestered state. Where God unmakes, but to remake the soul He else made first in vain; which must not be.

Always there will be the chance to turn and love and live. The nature of the soul demands it. The nature of God proclaims it. The compassion of Christ guarantees it.

We have the highest authority for believing that the Great Shepherd Himself will not be content if one of His sheep is missing from the final fold.

The Christian Agnostic: Leslie Weatherhead.

Songs of the Redeemed

An old legend puts the matter vividly:: A man dreamed one night that he was allowed to pass into the next world. When he arrived an angel invited him to visit heaven and hell. Together they went through all the courts of heaven, and the things they saw were very wonderful and very beautiful. But the heart of the visitor was ill at ease for he thought to himself, "This is all very fine, but how can they enjoy it while their brethren suffer in yonder torment?". And the angel read his very thoughts and said, "Would you like to see the place they call Hell?". And trembling a little the visitor said that he would. So it came to pass that they drew near the gates of hell. The flames were terrible and so great a heat was thrown out that the visitor thought, "We shall not get near enough to see anything". And again the angel read his thoughts and said "But can you hear nothing?" And to his surprise the visitor heard strange and beautiful music coming from the heart of the fire. And he said to his angelic guide, "Sir, tell me, what wondrous songs are those which the souls in hell are singing?" And the angel whispered softly in his ear, "They are the songs of the redeemed" he said.

The Christian Agnostic: Leslie Weatherhead.

Greater Love

A man who was entirely careless of spiritual things died and went to Hell. And he was much missed on earth by his old friends. His business manager went down to the gates of Hell to see if there were any chance of bringing him back. But though he pleaded for the gates to be opened, the iron bars never yielded. His cricket captain went also and besought Satan to let him out just for the remainder of the season. But there was no response. His minister went also and argued saying 'He was not altogether bad. Let him have another chance. Let him out just this once'. Many other friends of his went also and pleaded with Satan saying, 'Let him out. Let him out. Let him out'. But when his mother came, she spake no word of his release. Quietly, and with a strange catch in her voice, she said to Satan, *'Let me in'*. And immediately the great doors swung open upon their hinges. For love goes down through the gates of hell and there redeems the damned.

Author Unknown.

Found among the papers of a soldier killed in Ulster.
From a native American source. Given to me by
Reginald Willcock, Page to HM The Queen Mother.

Do not stand at my grave and weep
For I am not there
I do not sleep
I am a thousand winds that blow
I am a diamond glint on snow,
I am sunlight in ripened grain

I am the gentle falling rain,
When you waken in the morning hush
I am the silent uplifting rush,
Of quiet birds in circled flight.
I am the soft stars that shine in the night
do not stand at my grave and cry,
For I am not there
I did not die.

The Real Question

The real question before our death is not 'How much can I still accomplish or how much influence can I still exert?' but; 'How can I so live that I can continue to be fruitful when I am no longer here among my family and friends? that question shifts our attention from doing to being. Our doing brings success, but our being bears fruit. The great paradox of our lives is that while we are often very concerned about what we do, or still can do, we are most likely to be remembered for who we were. If it was the Spirit that guided our lives — the Spirit of love, joy, peace, gentleness, forgiveness, courage, perseverance, hope and faith — that Spirit that will not die but continues to grow from generation to generation.

Our Greatest Gift. A Meditation on
Dying and Caring: Henry J.M. Nouwen.

The Lighter Side

"Wrapped up in the thought of fellowship is that of humour. The power to worship, to use language, to be conscious of oneself, and to laugh, are the four great abilities which separate man from animals and show his divine nature. Here is the image of God. Joy and fellowship can hardly exist without laughter. God is revealed in Christ, and He again and again resorted to humour. God who presumably created the playfulness of kittens and puppies, must Himself rejoice when man uses this God-given faculty. Recently when a man died who always brought laughter to people's faces wherever he went, one mourner said to another, "There will be some fun somewhere in heaven tonight!". I do not suggest a heaven in which we gather as it were, in corners, and tell each other funny stories! But our humour here may well be a foretaste of the mirth and gaiety of the life above.

The Christian Agnostic: Leslie Weatherhead.

Life after Death

The life after death is thought of by Christians not as "ghost-ly", but as a real life, however greatly transformed, a life which is "far better" says St. Paul.

Then come the ordinary problems and questionings. Let us remember that "eye hath not seen, nor ear heard, the things which God has prepared for those who love him". This part of our theology is therefore partly agnostic, partly speculative, and properly tentative.

(a) The question of recognition. We cannot give a definite answer, but we can say that it would be a very strange Kingdom of Divine love in which you could neither find nor be found by those you loved best in this world.

(b) Our Lord says "in heaven they neither marry nor are given in marriage". Therefore presumably in a heavenly state of love there can be no kind of possessiveness, even of this kind. There must be a kind of contentedness with a reign of love which eliminates the need for dependence upon one person or another ... "All things are yours, and ye are Christ's and Christ is God's"

(c) I remember Martin Israel (who has second sight) telling me with calm and perfect conviction that a friend who had died suddenly (1) would not realise that he was dead; (2) would try to help those around him; (3) would then realise that he was "dead"; (4) would then enter into darkness — (5) which would become light, and in that light he would be met by those who were ready to lead him onwards. So Jesus says "in my Father's house there are many mansions" and mansions are resting places on a journey.

So (d) There is the idea of progress — let us not get bogged down by disputes about purgatory. The way of purgatory is *NOW*. Purgatory is already taking place. What a fuss there has been in the Synod about "prayers for the dead". The three stages of the body of Christ militant, expectant, triumphant — are not in succession but all the time one spiritual, mystical fact. In no kind of prayer are we trying to change God's mind. On All

Soul's day we meet with the departed in Christ who was raised from the dead and is the same yesterday, today and for ever.

(e) Is one 'farther on' than another? Is one at the top of the ladder and the other at the bottom? Is it a long long trail' and I shall never catch up with those that have gone before?' But surely the picture to work with is the circle, and 'progress' is entering more and more deeply into the centre, that is our Lord Jesus Christ himself, which we can do now, long before physical death; the picture to work with is *NOT* that of a long life with one miles ahead and another miles behind.

(f) The people question about the "great multitude which no man can number" — not only Christians — 'The mind boggles'. But we are men and women of finite mind and sight. There is no reason why Almighty God should not have room for all created beings.

The 'break' is death — the death of the body. We must resist as far as we can the recent death wish, but let us long for death to sin and lay hold on eternal life, long before the death of the body. And in the case of those who die very young or those who are mentally defective, presumably God who is the Lord of Life can cause them to grow and come to some kind of maturity though not in this world.

Eric Abbot

Death's Door

At death's door only one person can enter at a time. But it makes a great difference to know that on this side of the door there is a loving presence to accompany you and to prepare you for the presence that welcomes you on the other side. That seems to me the real mission of the new care-givers. In this field, to be that loving presence as fully and as humanly as possible.

Laurence Freeman.

The Typical Natural Death Experience

The experience begins with a feeling of easeful peace and a sense of well-being which soon culminates in a sense of overwhelming joy and happiness. This ecstatic tone, although fluctuating in intensity from case to case, tends to persist as a constant emotional ground as other features of the experience begin to unfold. At this point the person is aware that he feels no pain nor does he have any other bodily sensations. Everything is quiet. These cues may suggest to him that he is either in the process of dying or has already 'died'.

He then may be aware of a transitory buzzing or wind-like sound, but in any event he finds himself looking down on his physical body, as though viewing it from some external vantage point. At this time, he finds that he can see and hear perfectly; indeed his vision and hearing tend to be more acute than usual. He is aware of the actions and conversations taking place in the physical environment, in relation to which he finds himself in the role of a passive, detached spectator. All this seems very real — even quite natural — to him; it does not seem at all like a dream or an hallucination. His mental state is one of clarity and alertness.

At some point, he may find himself in a state of dual awareness. While he continues to be able to perceive the physical scene around him, he may also become aware of 'another reality' and feel himself being drawn into it. He drifts or is ushered into a dark void or tunnel and feels as though he is floating through it. Although he may feel lonely for a time, the experience here is predominantly peaceful and serene. All is extremely quiet and the individual is aware only of his mind and of the feeling of floating.

All at once, he becomes sensitive to but does not see, a presence. The presence who may be heard to speak or who may instead 'merely' induce thoughts into the individual's mind, stimulates him to review his life and asks him to decide whether he wants to live or die. This stock-taking may be facilitated by a rapid and visual playback of episodes from the person's life. At this stage he has no awareness of time or space, and the concepts themselves are meaningless. Neither is he any longer identified with his body. Only the mind is present and it is weighing, logically and rationally — the alternatives that confront him at this threshold separating life from death: to go further into this experience or to return to earthly life. Usually the individual decides to return on the basis, not of his own preference, but of the perceived needs of his loved ones, whom his death would necessarily leave behind. Once the decision is made, the experience tends to be abruptly terminated.

Sometimes, however, the decisional crisis occurs later or is altogether absent, and the individual undergoes further experiences. He may for example, continue to float through the dark void towards a magnetic and brilliant golden light, from which emanates a 'world of light' and preternatural beauty, to be (temporarily) reunited with deceased loved ones, before being told, in effect that it is not yet his time and that he has to return to life.

In any event, whether the individual chooses or is commanded to return to his earthly body and worldly commitments, he does return. Typically, however, he has no recollection how he has effected his 're-entry' for at this point he tends to lose all awareness. Very occasionally, however the individual may remember 'returning to his body' with a jolt or an agonizing wrenching sensation. He may even suspect that he re-enters 'through the head'. Afterward, when he is able to recount his experience, he finds that there are simply no words adequate to convey the feelings and quality of awareness he remembers. He may also be, or become reticent about discussing it with others, either because he feels no one will really be able to understand it or because he will be disbelieved or ridiculed.

Heading towards Omega: Kenneth Ring.

To Live Again

Helen Chappel White, the wife of a retired university president began searching out of her deep need when her elder son, a bomber navigator, was shot down over the Baltic Sea in 1944. A young chaplain supplied the first clue. The sorrowing mother had admitted that neither God nor prayer was real to her anymore.

"Then talk to your boy", the chaplain advised her. "Ask him to help you find and know God. He's closer to God now than you and I are — he'll lead you to Him".

The mother felt that nothing could be lost by trying. She began by setting aside a few minutes in her bedroom each morning, relaxing her body, quieting her mind, silently affirming her faith in the promise that her son was alive. She had no startling experiences. "I don't think that it is for 'signs and wonders' that this companionship across the line is permitted or should be cultivated", she wrote to me. But she has found more precious things — healing for her grief; a feeling of daily companionship with her boy; and at times a tossing of ideas back and forth amounting almost to conversation. "There's a solid, steadily growing core of utter reality in this spiritual companionship" she says. "Often just a kind of happy sharing ... I should not care to live at all without it any more; the past would hurt and the future terrify me.

Is There Life after Death?: Catherine Marshall.

A NEW JERUSALEM

To Mary, sister of Lazarus.

Jesus said to her "I am the resurrection and the life; he who believes in me, though he die, yet shall he live, and whoever lives and believes in me shall never die. Do you believe this?" She said to him, "Yes, Lord; I believe that you are the Christ, the Son of God, he who is coming into the world."

John 11: 25

The New Ghost

"And he casting away his clothes garment, rose and came
to Jesus."
And he cast it down, down, on the green grass,
Over the young crocuses, where the dew was —
He cast the garment of his flesh that was full of death
And like a sword his spirit showed out of the cold sheath.

He went a pace or two, he went to meet his Lord,
And, as I said, his spirit looked like a clean sword,
And seeing him the naked trees began shivering,
And all the birds cried out aloud as it were late spring.

And the Lord came on, He came down, and saw
That a soul was waiting there for Him one without flaw,
And they embraced in the churchyard where the robins
play,
And the daffodils hang down their heads as they burn
away.

The Lord held his head fast, and you could see
That He kissed the unsheeted Ghost that was gone free —

As a hot sun, on a March day, kisses the cold ground;
And the spirit answered, for he knew well that his peace
was found.

The spirit trembled, and sprang up at the Lord's word —
As on a wild April day springs a small bird —
So, the ghost's feet lifting him up, he kissed the Lord's
cheek.
And for the greatness of their love neither of them could
speak.

But the Lord went then, to show him the way
Over the young crocuses, under the green may
That was not quite in flower yet — to far distant land

Fredegond Shove

An African Creed

We believe in the one High God who out of love created the beautiful world and everything good in it. He created man and wanted man to be happy in the world. God loves the world and every nation and tribe on the earth. We have known this High God in the darkness and now we know him in the light. God promised in the book of his word, the bible, that he would save the world and all the nations and tribes.

We believe that God, made good his promise by sending his son, Jesus Christ, a man in the flesh, a Jew by tribe, born poor in a little village, who left his home and was always on safari doing good, curing people by the power of God, teaching about God and man, showing that the meaning of religion is love. He was rejected by his people, tortured and nailed hands and feet to a cross, and died. He lay buried in the grave, but the hyenas did not touch him, and on the third day he rose from the grave. He ascended to the skies. He is the Lord.

We believe that all our sins are forgiven through him. All who have faith in him must be sorry for their sins, be baptized in the Holy Spirit of God, live the rules of love and share the bread together in love, to announce the good news to others until Jesus comes again. We are waiting for him, He is alive. He lives. This we believe. Amen

Christianity Rediscovered. An Epistle from the Masai: Vincent J. Donovan.

Christianity Rediscovered

The prophet Micah heard the city of Jerusalem, the gathering place for all the tribes and nations crying aloud. He urged it to continue crying so that someone might respond to the cry. "Cry out, daughter of Zion," he said, "the Lord himself will hear you." The cry of Jerusalem is the cry of the city today. It is the cry of the church, the new Jerusalem. It is the cry of all the tribes and nations of the earth yearning to be filled at the messianic banquet table. The cry of Jerusalem is the cry of creation groaning and travailing even until now, waiting for the revelation of the sons and daughters of God. "Preach the gospel to all creation," Christ said. Are we only now beginning to understand what he meant? I believe the unwritten melody that haunts this book ever so faintly, the new song waiting to be sung in place of the hymn of salvation, is simply the song of creation. To move away from the theology of salvation to the theology of creation may be the task of our time.

Christianity Rediscovered. An Epistle
from the Masai: Vincent J. Donovan

The Flute

But let the final word on this great matter of the life of the world to come be not with the great preachers, not with the philosophers, not with the scholars of the scientists but with a child. She was dying, the twelve year old girl of this story, and recently in a London Children's hospital. During the weeks of her illness she had learned to pick out a few simple tunes on a flute which her parents had given her. One afternoon just before teatime in the ward, she had called to a nurse and said, "When I go to be with Jesus, don't forget to pack my flute. I know he'll want to hear me play my tune." Truly indeed did Christ say: "Whoever does not receive the Kingdom of God like a child shall not enter it."

A Time to Die: William Purcell.

Then I saw a new heaven and a new earth; for the first heaven and the first earth had passed away, and the sea was no more. And I saw the holy city, new Jerusalem, coming down out of heaven from God, prepared as a bride adorned for her husband, and I heard a great voice from the throne saying, "Behold, the dwelling of God is with men. He will dwell with them, and they shall be his people, and God himself will be with them; and he will wipe away every tear from their eyes, and death shall be no more neither shall there be mourning nor crying nor pain any more, for the former things have passed away.

Revelations 21: 1–5

Sources

p.23 Negro Spiritual

p.26 *The Natural Death Handbook*. Edited by Nicholas Albery, Jill Elliot and Joseph Elliot of the Natural Death Centre, 20 Heber Road, NW2 6AA.

p.29 *The Natural Death Handbook*. Edited by Nicholas Albery, Jill Elliot and Joseph Elliot of The Natural Death Centre.

p.30 A Universal Heart. *The Life and Vision of Brother Roger of Taizé: Kathryn Spink*. S.P.C.K.

p.31 *A Few Late Chrysanthemums*: John Betjeman. John Murray, London. Page 52

p.34 *Who Dies? An Investigation of Conscious Living and Conscious Dying*: Stephen Levine. Gateway Book Bath. Page 88

p.36 *I Dreamed of Africa*: Kuki Gallmann. Penguin, Page 213

p.38 *I Heard the Owl Call My Name*: Margaret Craven. Harrap. Page 70

p.43 *Common Ground*, Journal of Christians and Jews No 2, 1996.

p.46 *Common Ground*, Journal of the Christians and Jews No 1, 1995.

p.47 *Psalm 22*. The Study Bible. Eyre and Spottiiswoode.

p.48 *The Dance of Love*: Stephen Verney. Fob Paperbacks.

p.51 *Dead Man Walking*: Helen Prejean. HarperCollins. Pages 25-27

p.52 *Dead Man Walking*: Helen Prejean. HarperCollins. Page 48

p.53 *Dead Man Walking*: Helen Prejean. HarperCollins. Page 104

p.55 *The Light of Experience*—BBC 13th December 1976

p.56 *Requiem*: Margrit Dahn

p.57 *The Gates of Heaven*. The New Union Prayer Book.

p.58 *100 Personal Prayers*. Lutterworth Press. (No. 52) Page 29

p.59 *Architectural Apocalypse*: Ryjimoto

p.60 *Portrait of the Soviet Union*: Fitzroy Maclean. Weidenfeld and Nicholson.

p.61 Eva Heyman, German Catholic Nun. *Unveiled Nuns Talking*: Mary Loudon. 1992. Random House. Page 79

p.63 *Unveiled Nuns Talking*: Mary Loudon. Page 80

p.64 *Our Greatest Gift. A Meditation on Dying and Caring*: Henri J.M. Neuwen. Hodder and Stoughton. Page 56

p.66 Excerpts from a Sermon by Fr Mark Oakley. Preached at All Saints, Margaret St. 12th March 1995.

p.69 *I Heard The Owl Call My Name*: Margaret Craven. 1967. Harrap & Co. Pages 3&127

p.71 *With Open Heart*: Michael Quoist. Goldenbridge Gill and Macmillan. Dublin. No 43. Page 45

p.73 The Times: Melvin Bragg

p.75 *Death. The Final Stage of Growth*: Elizabeth Kubler-Ross. A Spectrum Book. Prentice Hall. London. Page 143

p.81 *Source Unknown*

p.82 *Death. The Final Age of Growth*: Elizabeth Kubler-Ross. Page 230

p.83 *With Open Heart*: Michael Quoist. Gill and Macmillan, Dublin. Page 107

p.84/85 *On Death and Dying*: Elizabeth Kubler-Ross. Tavistock Publications. 1970.

p.86 *Stray Birds*: Tagore. From Death and Dying by Elizabeth Kubler Ross. Page 246

p.87 *Dark Victory*: Martin Israel. Mowbray. 1995. Page 97

p.88 *Death. The Final Stage of Growth*: Elizabeth Kubler-Ross. A Spectrum Book. Prentice Hall International.

p.89 'Ode to a Nightingale': John Keats. Faber. Verses 6 and 7.

p.94 *Psalm 28*. The Study Bible.

p.95 *Flaming Feather*: Laurens Van der Post. Random House.

p.97 *Death. The Final Stage of Growth*: Elizabeth Kubler-Ross. A Spectrum Book. Prentice Hall International. London. 1975. Page 44

p.99 *On Death and Dying*: Elizabeth Kubler-Ross. Page 125

p.100 *Reflections in a Dusty Mirror*: Susan Wood. Page 15

p.101 *Creative Prayer*: Metropolitan Anthony of Sourozh. DLT.

p.103/104 *Dark Victory*: Martin Israel. Mowbray. Pages 60 & 72

p.105 *All In The End Is Harvest*. An Anthology For Those Who Grieve. Edited by Agnes Whitaker.

p.107 *Death. The Final Stage of Growth*: Elizabeth Kubler-Ross. A Spectrum Book. Prentice Hall International. Page 25

p.109 *On Death and Dying*: Elizabeth Kubler-Ross. Tavistock Publications. Page 7

p.115 *Holocaust Memorial Day with the Sisters of Sion.*

p.115/117/118 *The Tibetan Book of Living and Dying*: Sogyal Rinpoche. Rider. An Imprint of Random House. UK Ltd. Page 209, 212, 213

p.119 *A Walk With a White Bushman*: Laurens Van der Post. Penguin Books.

p.121 *An Investigation of Conscious Living and Conscious Dying*: Stephen Levine. Gasteway Books. Page 4

p.122 Many Smokes Magazine (now Wild Fire) Bear Tribe Medicine soc. WA 99209-9167 USA

p.124 *The Natural Death Handbook*. Edited by Nicholas Albery, Jill Elliot and Joseph Elliot, of The Natural Death Centre.

p.129 *Psalm 23*: The Study Bible.

p.130 *Acceptance*, Amy Carmichael, Dohnavur/CLC USA

p.131/140 *God for Nothing*: Richard MacKenna. Souvenir Press. Pages 141/142

p.132 *Death, The Inner Journey*: John Main. A talk given at the Fourth International Seminar on Terminal Care.

p.133 *Death. The Final Stage of Growth*: Elizabeth Kubler-Ross. A Spectrum Book. Prentice Hall International. London.

p.134 From an article written by Catherine C. Price.

p.136 *A Short Span of Days*: Laurence Freeman. Novalis. St Paul's University. Ottawa. 1991. Page 39

p.138 *The Celtic Vision*: Esther de Waal. Selections from The Carma Gedelica by Alexander Carmichael. Page 111

p.141 *Tears of Silence*: Jean Vanier. DLT.

p.145 *Tears of Silence*: Jean Vanier. DLT.

p.146 *Requiem*: Margrit Dahn.

p.148 *The Crucible of Suffering*: Ronald Blackburn.

p.149 *To You the Living*. Second Back Row Press. P.O. Box 43. Leura NSW 2781. Australia.

p.150 quoted in *From Beyond the Horizon*: Cicely Saunders. DLT. 1990.

p.154 Fairacres Oxford.

p.155 Ecclesiasticus. 44:9.10, 13-14. 'Dedicated to Those Which Have No Memorials'.

p.156 Hodder and Stoughton.

p.158 During the Retreat of the Blue Pilgrims. Alresford. July 26, 1996.

p.159 *With Open Heart*: Michael Quoist Gill & Macmillan. Dublin.

p.160 *The Divine Milieu*: Pierre Teilhard de Chardin. Editions du Seuil.

p.161 *Author Unknown.*

p.162 *A Return to Love*: Marianne Williamson. Reflections on the Principles of a Course in Miracles. HarperCollins.

p.163 *With Open Heart*: Michael Quoist. Gill and Macmillan. Page 37

p.165 *Journey for a Soul*. George Appleton. Fontana Books. 1974. William Collins & Son Ltd. Page 241

p.166 *With Open Heart*. Michael Quoist. Page 98

p.167 *Judge Not*, A Selection of Sermons: Eric James. 1978-1988.

p.168 *Markings*: Dag Hammerskjöld. Faber and Faber.

p.170 *Tao Te Ching*: Lao Tzu. Wildwood House Twenty Eight. A New Translation by Gia Fu Feng and Jane English.

p.171 Revelations 22:1-5. The Study Bible.

p.179 John: 20. The Study Bible.

p.180 *Beyond the Horizon*. Cicely Saunders. DLT.

p.181 *Mister God, This is Anna*: Fynn. HarperCollins.

p.182 *Our Greatest Gift. A Meditation on Dying and Caring*: Henri J.M. Nouwen. Hodder and Stoughton.

p.186 *A Time to Die*: William Purcell.Mowbrays. Page 88

p.187 *The Christian Agnostic*: Leslie Weatherhead.

p.188 *A Return to Love*: Marianne Williamson. HarperCollins.

p.189 *The Celtic Vision*. Esther de Waal.

p.195 Luke 24: 13-25. The Study Bible.

p.196 *Prayer and The Pursuit of Happiness*. Richard Harries. Fount Paperbacks. Page 45.

p.198. *Author Unknown.*

p.199 *Prayer and the Pursuit of Happiness*: Richard Harries. Page 30

p.200 *Anonymous.*

p.201 *The Christian Agnostic*: Leslie Weatherhead. A. James Page 232

p.202 *So This is Death*: G.A.G. Bowden. The Undiscovered Country. Edmund Robert Morgan. Published by Edward Arnold.

p.203 Arthur Bryant's Biography.

p.205/206/208 *The Testimony of Light*. Helen Greaves. Neville Spearman. Pages 107/108/56

p.209 *Saga of King Olaf*: Henry Wadsworth Longfellow.

p.211/213/214 *Revelation. Letters from the Other Side of Death*: General Lord Rawlinson. Edgar Dunstan.

p.217 John 20:24-29. The Study Bible.

p.218 *Our Greatest Gift. A Meditation on Dying and Caring*: Henri J.M. Nouwen.

p.220/221 *The Christian Agnostic*: Leslie Weatherhead.

p.222 *Author Unknown.*

p.224 *Our Greatest Gift*. A Meditation on Dying and Cling: Henri J.M. Nouwen.

p.225 *The Christian Agnostic*: Leslie Weatherhead. Page 233

p.230 *Heading Towards Omega*: Kenneth Ring. The Natural Death Handbook. Page 41

p.231 *Is There Life After Death?* Catherine Marshall. From To Live Again. Fontana Books. Page 227

p.235 John 11:25. The Study Bible.

p.237/238 *Christianity Rediscovered. An Epistle from the Masai*: Vincent J. Donovan.

p.239 *A Time to Die*: William Purcell. Mowbrays. Page 149

p.240 Revelations 21:1-5

Index

Christian Meditation Centres

International Centre: 23 Kensington Square London W8 5HN United Kingdom.
Tel: +44 171 937 4679
Fax: +44 171 937 6790
E-mail:
wccm@compuserve.com

Australia: Australian Christiin Mediti1tion Community
PO Box 66390
St. Kilda Rd. Central Victoria 3004.
Tel/Fax: +61 7 3300 3873
or +61 3 9435 8943
E-mail:
acmchll@Bigpond.com

Belgium: Christelijk Medititie Centrum Beiaardlaan 1
1850 Grimbergen.
Tel/Fax: +32 2 269 5071

Canada: Christian Meditation Community
PO Box 55, Station NDG Montre
Quebec H4A 3P9.
Tel: +1 514 766 0475
Fax: +1 514 937 8178
E-mail:
mark.schofield@sympitico.ca

Centre de Méditation Chrétienne
Cap Vie, 367 boul. Ste Rose Laval QC H71 1N3.
Tel/Fax: +1 514 625 0133

Germany: Zentrum für Christiche Meditation
c/o Gunter Meng
Postfach 122045
68071 Minnheim.
Tel: +49 171 268 6245
Fax: +49 40 3603 095 720
E-mail: GueMeng@aol.com

Ireland: Christian Meditation Centre
4 Elbana Ave.
Dun Laoghare
Co. Dublin.
Tel: +353 1 280 1505
Fax: +353 1 280 8720

Italy: Centro di Meditazione Chritiana
Abbazia di San Miniato al Monte
Via Delle Porte
Sante 34
50125 Firenze.
Tel/Fax: +39 55 247 6302

New Zealand: Christian Meditation Centre
PO Box 35531
Auckland 1310.

United Kingdom:
Christian Meditation Centre The Hermitage
Monastery of Christ the King
29 Bramley Road
Cockfosters
London N14 4HE.
Tel/Fax: +44 181 441 0680
E-mail:cmcuk@ucompuserve.com.

United States: Christian
Meditation Centre
1080 West Irving Park Rd
Roselle IL 60172.
Tel/Fax: +1 630 351 2613

John Main Institute
7315 Brookville Rd.
Chevy Chase
MD 20815.
Tel:+ 1 301 6528635
E-mail: wmcoerp@erols.com

Christian Meditation Centre
1619 Wight St.
Wall
NJ.07719
Tel: +1 732 681 6238
Fax: +1 732 280 5999
E-mail: gjryan@aol.com

The Cornerstone Centre
1215 East Missouri Ave.
Suite A 100
Phoenix AZ. 85014-2914.
Tel: +1 602 279 3454
Fax: +1 602 957 3467
E-mail:
ecrmjr@worldnet.att.net